Time Mana

Handbook for Lawyers

How-to Tactics That Really Work

Gary Richards

ISBN: 0615782434

ISBN 13: 9780615782430

------*DEDICATION*------

*To my wife, Linda, whose loving, unerring instincts
need no 'handbook'.*

✗ ✗ ✗

How to Use This Book

This book is called a "Handbook" because it fits the common definition as a...:

"... reference book in a particular field."

That's what it is. By using the table of contents, you can pick it up and find information on almost any time management topic that you would like to review. That makes it easy to quickly find suggested tactics and compare those to your present tactics if you are seeking improvement.

If you are an experienced professional, I suggest you use the handbook approach and troubleshoot any habits you might want to revise or refresh. Just use the table of contents to locate any specific elements of time management you want to revisit.

But, if this is the first time you have thought seriously about the more exact discipline of time management, you could read it from cover to cover, making notes on sections that particularly appeal to you. You will find much here of help.

I recall the first time I dived in to the subject almost 40 years ago. I had just gotten a bad performance review from a partner in our global accounting firm. I oversaw engagements where we billed fees by the hour, as you do, (and as I have done ever since). But, in order to 'get it all done well', I was coming in to the office early, skipping lunch, leaving late and often working on weekends. That partner gave me high marks on the *quality* of my work. However, as to my *process* for getting it done, he used the tennis analogy of "...

running around a weak backhand..." to illustrate my need to "...get better organized so I could take less time and have less stress..." doing that good work.

My resulting professional development assignment was to "get organized"! So I acquired training in time management from Dr. Alec Mackenzie, author of <u>The Time Trap</u>. It turned my career around. After 5 years successfully using my improved personal organization, I left and started my own consultancy, and affiliated with Mackenzie as an associate for a few years.

Since then, I have taught the subject thousands of times, mainly to lawyers. During those interactions, I have tested the validity of my methods, and picked up many great additional tips from successful attorneys. I hope you too can benefit from these collected techniques and insights that *"Really work!"*

...GR

You can see more about Gary Richards on the last page of this book and on the back cover.

✗ ✗ ✗

Table of contents

❧ ❧ ❧

Chapter 1

How to Manage Yourself, Not Time

"My father was a lawyer too, and he taught me that if I learn the law, show up every day, and work hard for my clients, I'll be a big success. I've done that for 10 years as a partner....but, lately it is just not working!"

SAID BY A LAWYER BEING COACHED ON
IMPROVING PERSONAL EFFECTIVENESS.

It is challenging to manage our time because at some level we actually realize that *we can't manage it.*

Characteristics of Time

This idea is easier to grasp and act on by first thinking through some of the characteristics of time[1]:

- Equally distributed-everyone has the same amount of time
- Unstorable-Can't save or store it. Use it, or lose it!

---

1 Adapted from: Mackenzie, Alec, *Time Management (course workbook)* 1980, p. 14. *(Out of print.)*and Drucker, Peter. *The Effective Executive.* New York, New York: Harper Collins, 2002. P 26 Print.

- Invariable-Moves at a fixed rate
- Irretrievable-It can't be recovered
- Limited-can't create more of it
- Limitless-was passing before we arrived, during our whole life and will continue after we're gone
- Indivisible-everything we think, say or do takes time
- Uncontrollable-it can't be managed. We just manage ourselves while it passes.

So, what we CAN manage is ourselves. The core objective of managing ourselves is to:
- Spend enough time
- On the right thing
- At the right time

In other words, <u>manage priorities</u>. Be efficient on tasks of high relative importance, and don't get trapped in the more trivial tasks instead. This book is about specific practices to help you do just that.

What takes your time, but contributes little?

The classic approach to improving 'time management' is to first, identify your timewasters, i.e., those things that take your time, but either do *not contribute* to your priorities for that period, or *interfere with completing* your priorities. Here are the eight timewasters that lawyers mention most[2] to me (not in order of priority):
- Lack of objectives/priorities/planning
- Unrealistic time estimates/ attempting too much
- Interruptions from others: telephone, drop-ins.
- Personal disorganization, cluttered desk/office
- Untrained/inadequate staff

---

2 Unpublished study of lawyer time logs by Alec Mackenzie and Gary Richards 1981-2002. Study continued by Richards to 2013.

- Poor delegation/involving myself too much in routine tasks
- Don't follow up enough
- Over-responding to emails, instant messaging and voice mails

This book will offer ideas that address most of these habits that interfere with reaching the results you want.

The three key questions you must ask about your time according to Peter Drucker[3] are:

1. Am I giving the right <u>kind</u> of time to the really important things? (The right <u>amount</u> of time, at the <u>right time, uninterrupted.</u>)
2. What is taking my time and contributing little to my objectives?
3. What would happen if I didn't do it? (If nothing, be ruthless and cut it out).

When you say "yes" to one task, you are saying "no" to everything else in your life for that moment. So make that "yes" choice pay.

The lawyers' dilemma

Another challenge for a lawyer is how to be effective AND efficient: How to bill as many hours as I can without being inefficient in reaching the clients' desired results.

Consider these definitions:

<u>Efficiency</u>: Doing things right.
<u>Effective</u>: Doing the right things right.

For purposes of this book, <u>*lawyer effectiveness*</u> *in managing a client matter* is considered to be:

---

3 Drucker, Peter. The Effective Executive. New York, New York City: Harper Collins, 2002. P.156. Print.

"Getting the clients' desired results by incurring no more fees than absolutely necessary to efficiently get that result."

This means that the client would NOT be expected to pay for the lawyer's inefficiencies. Conversely, if the work is required to efficiently get the clients' desired result, the client WOULD be expected to pay for it, unless other relational issues override.

Some of the benefits of good time management are:
- Increased client satisfaction
- Higher realization
- Increased competitiveness in getting new business

The core of "Time Management" is managing yourself to stay focused on your priorities (See **Chapter 3. How to Benefit From a Written Daily Plan**). So a good core question to address is this one:

"How can I better manage myself and my tasks during the day?"

If you have had thoughts like those below, you may have an opportunity to improve managing yourself and your tasks within the day:
- *I'm not billing a high enough percentage of the hours I am working.*
- *I come in early, or leave late, or skip lunch (and work on weekends?) or all the above…just have too much to get done, not enough time to do it!*
- *Interruptions keep me from getting done what I should.*
- *I seem to jump from one case, task, matter to another without really homing in on any one thing to conclusion.*
- *Deadlines seem to creep up on me making me pull longer days just to get things done on time.*

If those thoughts are familiar, use a simple system with three basic practices for a powerful, personal time management system:

- Keep a To Do List
- Do a Written Daily Plan-it takes 10 minutes a day
- Beef up use of your calendar

Also see the *Appendix 1. How to Take and Analyze a Time Log* if you are serious about identifying exactly what time wasters may be affecting you. After all, a well-stated problem is half solved! Also, if you want to review causes and solutions for key time wasters of lawyers, see the *Appendix 3. Time Waster Analyses: Causes and Solutions.*

How to use the Pareto Principle

Keep in mind that the Pareto Principle (80/20 rule[4]) probably applies to your daily tasks, your client mix etc.

Figure 1: 80/20 Rule

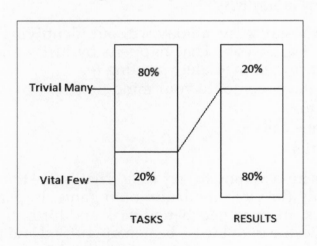

4 Pareto, Vilfredo; Page, Alfred N. (1971), Translation of *Manuale di economia politica ("Manual of political economy")*, A.M. Kelley, ISBN 978-0-678-00881-2

That rule means that a small percentage of your clients are probably giving you the bulk of your income; a small percentage of your daily tasks give you the bulk of your results, as shown in **Figure 1**. So, the challenge is to focus on those "vital few" things that give the bulk of the results, and ignore the "trivial many". You've heard it called "working smart".

Lee Iacocca[5] put it this way:

"If you want to make good use of your time, you've got to know what's most important and then give it all you've got."

But, effectiveness drops sharply if you focus too much on the "trivial many" 80% of your possible tasks.

Why It Is Easy To Stay 'Busy'

It is easy to 'stay busy' all day without identifying the vital few tasks facing you. That happens by just walking into your office and immediately reacting to:
- whatever comes to your mind first
- visitors
- phone calls
- emails

It takes no planning to stay *busy*. That is like the bird that accidentally flies into the badminton game. In place of the shuttlecock, the bird gets batted back and forth. By the end of the game, the poor bird is beaten up, ruffled and tired, but no closer to its destination. Are some days like that for you?

Chapters two through five describe a proven set of practices you can adopt or improve upon to get you better

---

5 Ioacocca, Lee. *Ioacocca, An Autobiography*. New York, N.Y.: Bantam Dell, 1984. Print, Page 21.

"organized" and make you a better "time manager" by focusing more robustly on your true priorities.

Your reward is that you can free up some time to re-purpose to whatever you choose: more family time, improve your own fitness, develop more business, relax, go to the theater, take a longer vacation....your choice!

✄ ✄ ✄

Chapter 2

How to Get the Most from Your To Do List

The best tool to help you remember tasks you need to do is a 'To Do List'. Most lawyers keep To Do Lists, but, as in any skill, there are effective ways to use them, and not so effective ways to use them. This section explains a simple and easy way to manage a To Do List so you won't forget important tasks that occur to you when doing something else. If you are already a 'To Do List' star, you can skip this section. But scan it before you abandon it, as there may be a nugget or two you can add to your own method of managing your To Do List.

Why a To Do List?

Confucius is supposed to have said:

> *"The palest ink is more reliable than the most powerful memory."*

If you write down a task you don't want to forget, you can always find it. If you don't write it down when it occurs to you, it is at risk of being forgotten. Some subtle notions are irrecoverable if not captured when they first strike you. Without writing them, you may not be able to recall them.

In short, a To Do List is like a bucket into which you just toss things as you think of them to be looked at and planned later. Think of it as a memory substitute or a memory annex.

If you have ever been startled as you are falling asleep with a thought like *"…Oh no…I forgot to…"* or *"…Oh boy…I hope I remember to….."* you can immediately see the value of writing down any important task immediately when it occurs to you. A To Do List can help you avoid anxiety over forgetting the important but undone.

So, the reason for a To Do List is to help you dependably locate important tasks you thought of when you were too busy on something else to take action on them. Storing them on a To Do List allows you to work them into your plans or take action on them as they become a priority.

What EXACTLY is a To Do List?

A To Do List is a list of tasks that you don't want to forget to do, accumulated over time as you think of them, usually with no deadline for completion:

- It is what you don't want to forget
- It is not a plan, it is a list
- It is a substitute memory or a *'memory annex'*
- If it is on your list, you will never forget it
- You can always choose to do it or not do it, but you won't forget it
- The To Do List reduces your anxiety over forgetting important tasks that are yet undone

Keep your To Do List in any continuously available place. For example:

- Your smart phone's memo app. Easy to open and access. It is an especially *efficient* place if your phone has dictation capability (iPhone 4S, 5, etc.). That way, you can simply enter a new to-do by speaking it into your smart phone!
- A Word or Excel file that is easily accessible works fine.
- A dedicated legal pad that you always have with you. Retro, but can work just fine!

Of course, any electronic version is easier than a pen and paper version to delete, copy, paste, re-sequence, etc.

Any task that you *don't want to forget* is written on the To Do List. That habit creates a list over time that you can refer to at any time in the future when planning, or when you get a windfall of time unexpectedly.

If an event or task is already scheduled in your calendar, it doesn't go on the To Do List because appearing in your calendar's reminder alert will remind you (more on calendars in **Chapter 4. How to Get More from Your Calendar**). List only *unscheduled tasks* on your To Do List.

How To Make Your To Do List More Efficient

The best tip is to keep only one To Do List as a comprehensive view of all pending tasks...business tasks and personal tasks. But here are some other workable tips:

Remove a task from the To Do List when it is either:
- Done, or
- Prioritized in your Written Daily Plan, or
- Delegated, or
- Determined to be not worth doing

Write the estimated time you think each task will take as you add it to the To Do List. That helps when deciding whether to do it when you have some down/found time, or when adding it to your daily plan. The estimated duration gives it more definition. Also, this is good practice at estimating task duration, an important learned skill.

Keep your To Do List in sections if you deal with enough complexity: *Work, Business Development, Family, Personal Business, Health*, etc. But look out....keep it simple. The To Do List is to be a tool, not a separate *project*.

Put the task on the To Do List for a specific day, week or month if the task is best done within a certain specific day, week or month. That way, it won't clutter up your more immediate tasks, but you'll see it when you start to plan its day, week or month.

Keep the list segmented by person if you deal with a number of the same people continuously, such as your staff or matter team. That way, when you do talk with them (or they contact you), your list of tasks, questions or assignments for them is immediately available to add to the discussion if time permits. (See more about this in **Chapter 5** at *How to Use Team Logs*.)

Not everything on your To Do List has to be done. If a task on your To Do List continues to be ignored because it is just never important enough to acct on or to include in a Written Daily Plan, or to delegate, then maybe it doesn't need to be done at all! Things change...it is amazing what the world can get along without!

✗ ✗ ✗

Chapter 3

How to Benefit from a Written Daily Plan

Yes, *written*. I know, as a lawyer, you are perfectly capable of thinking through your day in just seconds. But, by *writing* down your plan (in the calendar, a word or excel document, legal pad, etc…it doesn't matter where), you *refine your thinking* by selecting the words to write. That simply does not occur when left to thinking alone. Plus, when written, you can make quick reference to it during the day, and even show it to those who need to know what you are involved in that day. So yes, a <u>Written </u>Daily Plan. Lee Iacocca[6] put it this way:

> *"As I learned from McNamara, the discipline of writing something is a step toward making it happen… But, there's something about putting your thoughts on paper that forces you to get down to specifics. That way it's harder to deceive yourself – or anybody else."*

And yes, *daily*. It becomes the handle on events that help steer you through whatever comes up throughout the day. Each day is different, and has its own priorities you need to manage for *that day*. So yes, a Written <u>Daily </u>Plan.

---

6 Ioacocca, Lee. *Page 50.*

Also, yes *plan*. No one wants to spend too much time planning and be accused of having "paralysis of analysis". But most lawyers don't have that problem.

Most lawyers would rather get something done than plan to get something done. That sense of urgency is one of the characteristics that sometimes helps you make things happen in your practice when there is an emergency, or there is no time but to act. But consistently diving in to your day without a plan could be evidence of the *Activity Priority Syndrome: Given a choice between planning and acting, you choose to act.*

To establish both the urgency to act, and clarity of priorities, do a Written Daily *Plan*.

The following easy steps are how to take 5-10 minutes to write your daily plan, EACH DAY.

First, decide when the best time is for you to plan your day. Some find it better to plan the next day as the last thing you do before leaving the office each day. Others prefer to plan the day as the first thing you do upon arriving at your desk each morning. Consistency is the point, so make it a daily 'ritual' at the same time of day to get the best results.

List everything that you can think of that you would *like* to get done this day.

Just write down each task as you think of it, starting with its verb: "*Locate* the Adams mortgage document... research... find.... call...email...schedule....etc."

Refer also to your To Do List (more on that below) and include any tasks from that list that you want to do this day.

Capture this list on a legal pad, Word doc, or Excel... whatever is most comfortable for you, listing the important tasks for the day as they come to mind.

<u>Estimate how long each task will take.</u>

If you have ever underestimated a client's fee or had to change an expected deadline, you know the importance of durations. Like any skill, one gets better at estimating task durations with practice.

So, start practicing daily by estimating the time required to complete each task on the list of your Written Daily Plan. Just take a stab, off the top of your head....you may be surprised how long your list will take, and it is important to know that at the start of your day. So, estimate the duration of each task, write the estimate by each task, and total the result as shown below in **Figure 2.**

Figure 2: Written Daily Plan-DRAFT

Priority	Task	Est. Hrs.
	Locate & review Adams mortgage document	1 .0
	Schedule meeting with Randall	.5
	Talk with Mattie's soccer coach about how she got injured.	.75
	Work on AnyCorp	1.0
	Call Rachel re: outcome of Hong Kong call	1.5
	Assign patent search to Raj	1.0
	Plan wrap-up meeting with Topcorp, and schedule.	1.25
	EST. TOTAL TIME	7.0

CAUTION: Don't *over plan* your day. You need to leave some time in your day *unplanned* so you can be available for the unexpected but important items that always "come up". So, think about this, and decide how many hours you can safely commit to 'planned tasks' each day, and how many hours you must leave open and unplanned so you can be available for the unknown but important things that will undoubtedly arise.

How to assign priorities

By *"Assign priorities…"* is meant *"…place a ranking of relative value to each task…"*. Notice, a *priority* rank is assigned *relative to all the other tasks on the list for the same time period,* not an absolute value. That is why you list all tasks you would like to get done for the day *BEFORE* you prioritize them.

Of course, if you had enough time to get everything done every day, there would be no need to set priorities – just show up and work a full day and go home with everything having been accomplished! But most lawyers can't get everything done that comes to their mind in a day, so it's necessary to set priorities. Do it for each day the night before or first thing in the morning.

This is where a little pretending can be a powerful tactic. Ask yourself the key question in setting priorities:

*"If I could do **ONLY ONE** of these tasks by the end of day, which would it be?"*

Put a '1' next to that task at its left, creating a 'priority' column as shown below in **Figure 3**.

Of course, you may well be able to actually do *all the tasks* by day's end, but this 'pretend' drill gets to the bottom of what is *relatively* most important. Making yourself answer this question forces you to assign it a value relative to all else on the list.

Now repeat the question, but change the priority number each time until all are 'ranked':

"If I *could do* **ONLY TWO** *tasks today, what would the second one be?" (Rank it to its left)*

And

"If I *could do* **ONLY THREE**….*etc."(Rank it)*

So, in a couple of minutes, your daily plan will look something like **Figure 3**, showing your priority decisions in the left column:

Figure 3: Written Daily Plan with Priorities

Priority	Task	Est. Hrs.
3	Locate & review Adams mortgage document	1 .0
4	Schedule meeting -Randall	.5
2	Talk with Mattie's soccer coach about how she got injured.	.75
1	Work on AnyCorp (*see its matter plan*)	1.0
6	Call Rachel re: outcome of Hong Kong call	1.5
5	Assign patent search to Raj	1.0
7	Plan wrap-up meeting with Topcorp, and schedule.	1.25
	Est. Total Time	7.0

Two more valuable insights appear in the above example:
- The resulting *#1 priority for this day is the FOURTH task that occurred to you as you made the list.* That demonstrates that often the *most important task for the day* is NOT the first task that comes to mind. So, setting priorities this way improves your focus on priorities versus starting with the first important thing that comes to mind…it may not be the MOST important, as this demonstrates.

- Also, the number 1 priority, *"Work on AnyCorp'*, will require that you refer to the matter plan for AnyCorp that was done earlier. The work tasks in that plan appear in that matter plan document, NOT in your Daily Plan. That is how longer-term matter plans associate with the Daily Plan. Also, see **Figure 4: How Matter Plans Associate with Written Daily Plans.** (Specific tips on matter planning are found in *Chapter 7: How to Write a Task Level Matter Plan and Budget*.)

NOTE: The *criteria you use* for setting priorities is highly individual to you, the time period that you are planning and your specific situation. Each time you set priorities, the criteria could be any number of salient characteristics of the task being evaluated, such as whether the task:

- Is linked to a Goal of your Practice Area or Firm (See Appendix 4: *Planning Model for a Law Practice*)
- Has the earliest deadline
- Has the greatest cost to the firm if not handled
- Could generate the greatest profit to the firm if handled
- Is the oldest matter
- Is an over-due expectation of an important client
- Has the best chance for new business

You will intuitively assign some criteria or combination of criteria when you force yourself to answer the question *"If I can only do one thing what would it be?"* for the day being planned.

How to work your Daily Plan

"Think of many things; do one." – Portuguese proverb

Now you can go to work on the #1 priority until it is complete, and then go right to #2 and so on. It is a good feeling to have the track to work on already decided.

Also, if you have written this plan in either Excel or Word, you can easily use the 'sort' function to sort the task list by the priority column[7] to reorder the list by priority rank. The daily plan is a little easier to use when viewed in priority sequence since you can start at the top, and work down the list during the day.

Regardless of how you sequence your list, the priorities for the day have been decided and written, and are ready to tackle in the right (for you) order!

NOTE: It is often NOT possible to begin immediately on the #1 priority because you need input or decisions from another, such as your client or another lawyer, the file clerk, or an associate. So go to #2 or the first one where you have what you need to start work immediately.

Then, you can begin on the #1 priority just as soon as what you were waiting for is received.

As you complete each prioritized task, check it off. That is a good way to record/recognize your progress as you go through the day. The prioritized plan list helps focus your efforts and shows the results.

As other things come up that were not on your plan, you can compare their importance to the item you are working on to see if you should defer the new task, or interrupt and handle the new task if it is more important than what you are working on. So, the Written Daily Plan helps you continue to make priority decisions all day long. (More in **Chapter 5. How to Manage Interruptions** on why it is a must to know

---

7 In Word or Excel, select all rows under the heading row that are ranked. In Word, click on "Format/ A->Z Sort". In Excel, click on "Data/ A->Z Sort".

your priorities for the day in order to manage interruptions effectively.)

Starting each day with a clear set of priorities in the form of your Written Daily Plan creates momentum and reduces stress. Sure, there are some reasons that even when you have identified the number one priority, you may not be motivated to tackle it:

- It is a huge task and will require a lot of time (also a reason to start on it early in the day!)
- It may involve interactions that are likely to be tense or include conflict. (No one likes to *"pet the porcupine"*)
- It involves uncertainties
- It may require knowledge you don't have

Your Written Daily Plan emboldens you to focus on the decision you have just made about a task's relative importance. It's a bit like the old admonition about pie: "eat the crust first – the filling will be your reward». So, do the tough, most important one first, and the remainder of your list is more pleasurable by contrast.

How to end your day

When your workday is done, you can do three meaningful things with your Written Daily Plan:

- Review the tasks you have completed (checked off) as an indication of how well (or poorly) you stuck to priorities. It would be stressful to come to the end of the day and feel that the number one priority had not gotten enough attention.
- Move undone tasks to the next day. If a ranked task didn't get done, it probably should appear again on tomorrow's plan unless priorities have shifted. William James put it this way:

"Nothing is so fatiguing as the eternal hanging on of an uncompleted task."

- <u>Compare the *actual time* each completed task took ver-sus *your initial estimate* for it</u>. When you enter your chargeable time for the day in your time system, you can easily do this. With this daily comparison, you'll get a lot better at estimating task durations.

How matter plans fit into your Written Daily Plan

As mentioned elsewhere, matter plans list all the tasks necessary to complete the work promised to that client as shown below in **Figure 4**. So, there is no need to repeat writing those steps in either your calendar or your Written Daily Plan. It is sufficient to simply reference the matter plan as a single item on the Written Daily Plan as shown below in **Figure 4**.

Figure 4: How Matter Plans Associate
with Written Daily Plans

	Written Daily Plan: Tues.			Matter Plan for AnyCorp LLC	
1	Work on AnyCorp	1.0	1	_____ _____	☑
2	Talk with Mattie's soccer coach about how she got injured.	.75	2	_____ _____	☑
3	Locate & review Adams mortgage document	1.0	3	_____ _____	☑
4	Schedule meeting with Randall	0.5	④	_____ _____	

When beginning work on that first item on your Written Daily Plan, you simply go to *The Matter Plan for AnyCorp LLC* and work on its next undone task (the first one without a ☑), 4, until it is done, or your planned one-hour work period ends. Continue working on the next tasks in order until your scheduled one-hour period is over. In the matter plan, check off the tasks you have completed in the right-hand column and return to your Written Daily Plan, *"Talk with Mattie's soccer..."*.

✄ ✄ ✄

Chapter 4

How to Get More from Your Calendar

Your calendar is probably the easiest time management tool and the most intuitive to use.

This section is a review of some basics with a few not-so-obvious improvement tips.

Enter matter work periods in your calendar

When a client matter plan is completed (**Chapter 7-How to Improve Matter Management**), schedule work periods for its tasks in your calendar far enough in advance of task due dates to complete them on time. Include follow-ups with others if you are the matter leader or are working interdependently on some task for that client.

An "appointment with yourself" time-activates the work and increases the likelihood that you will not put off working on that matter. Such an "appointment with yourself" in your calendar also positions you to better protect time for that work when other tempting things "come up".

How to use appointments with yourself

You may also need to sustain effort in key categories of tasks that never make it to the top priority on your To Do List, but nonetheless should command periodic, repeated attention. So make an appointment with yourself periodically for those special types of work, such as:
• Business Development
• Filing
• Staff meetings
• Planning

Put helpful details with the event entry

Confirmed events, tentative events (place-holders) and *appointments* are the primary items to put on your calendar. Put them there *just as soon as you commit* to them or decide to save time for them.

Most electronic calendars have important and helpful fields for the following information for each event:
• Name of event
• Location of the event
• Name of the Person(s) attending
• Time the event begins & ends
• How often the event is to be repeated, if it is
• Alerts/reminders: how far in advance, how many (these *external stimuli* to remind you are a relief from having to *remind yourself* that the meeting is coming up).
• Notes: References to documents needed, who initiated the meeting, etc…anything to jog your understanding of the event

TIP: Also in the 'Notes' field, enter phone number(s) of key contacts(s) involved in/affected by the appointment. Sure, you might have their phone numbers in your contact records, but having phone numbers right in the calendar entry saves you a 'look-up' step should questions emerge or should you want to make a change in the date or agenda.

TIP: Enter the "date committed" for events that are entered far into the future (i.e., 3 months or more out). For example say that on January 11th you agree to host a quarterly matter review session with your Anycorp matter team on April 16. Write *"Agreed to 1/11"*in the calendar event notes for April 16. Knowing how long you have been committed to an event is one important factor in your willingness to cancel it or keep it should another event arise to compete for that same time.

How to use the "R.O.F.R." entry for pending commitments from others

R.O.F.R. stands for "Right of First Refusal". Say that your client Anycorp asks you to present something at their board meeting. The date for the board meeting is yet to be determined, but it will probably be held *either* the first or second Tuesday of March. To calendar this indeterminate arrangement, you would give the client an ROFR for the 5th *and* the 12th of March. So, the entry in your calendar on March 5 *and* March 12 would be:

(ROFR) Anycorp board meeting (3/5 or 3/12?)

That means that if you later receive a request for, say the 5th from a different client, Allmoney, Inc. but before Anycorp had decided their date, you would check with Anycorp before committing to Allmoney. If AnyCorp hasn't committed to it yet, you could explain your need and decide whether to commit it to Allmoney Inc. or keep holding it for AnyCorp. If you decide to give it to Allmoney, it is so calendared; everyone is on the same page.

How to use "meeting x 3" scheduling

Have you ever had one of those days with back-to-back meetings? If so, you will recall not being able to follow up on those meetings immediately because of the need to race to the next meeting. Also, your preparation for the next meeting might have been reduced beyond what you would prefer. Here's a suggestion: *Use the Meeting x 3 method when* scheduling most meetings.

Here's why and how: You normally need to *prepare* for a scheduled meeting, and probably need to *follow it up* afterward. So, why not schedule *three* time periods in your calendar:

1. Time to *prepare for the meeting* –say 30 minutes, calendared for a day or two *before* the meeting day
2. Time to *attend* the actual meeting, of course
3. Time to *follow up* the meeting outcomes-like immediately after the meeting. That's when the details and nuanced outcomes are the freshest. The longer you wait to follow up, the more likely it is to overlook an important subtlety.

That way, the time to prepare and follow up the meeting are elevated to "appointments", the same level of importance as the meeting. It is easier to 'protect' time for them just like you protect time for the scheduled meeting itself!

The "Meeting x 3" approach to scheduling in your calendar can improve your preparation and participation at the meeting, ensure solid follow up, reduce your stress, and make your meetings more meaningful.

How to use shared calendaring to advantage

If your organization allows all lawyers to see each other's calendars (Google, Outlook Enterprise, etc.), use it to advantage. Of course, no one should be given the permission to *enter or change* your calendar, except your assistant within limited parameters. By "sharing" is meant the ability for each lawyer's calendar to show each other lawyer categories of unavailability, like 'busy', 'out of town', 'client conference' etc.

That way, when you want to plan a conference call, WebEx, meeting, etc. you can do a 'busy search' for uncommitted slots in the calendars for each person to be invited BEFORE sending the invitation. The likelihood of their availability is greatly increased and you avoid having to "shop" a date by sending numerous invitations to narrow it down based on individual responses.

✄ ✄ ✄

Chapter 5

How to Manage Interruptions

"We have an open door policy in our firm. After all, if someone needs me enough to show up at my door, it must be important to them, so I better stop what I'm doing and take it! Plus, answering my own phone is just the personal touch our firm wants to convey to clients, so when it rings, I answer. I also like being able to email or text message whenever I think of it regardless of what I'm doing. "

There is an element of logic and good intentions in those statements. But living by them can be a disaster, and will defeat most lawyers. Why is that? Because without some way to compare priorities of these interruptions with the priority of what you are engaged in when they occur, time will likely be spent on some less important tasks, delaying or ignoring more important tasks.

One cannot, and should not, *eliminate* all interruptions, of course. Some interruptions are why you are in business as a lawyer! But effectively eliminating the <u>unnecessary</u> interruptions and managing the <u>necessary</u> ones are vital skills in managing your priorities and delivering diligent legal service, with less stress.

You may already have some tactics in place to help you avoid interruptions. A common one is to start coming in early to your office or staying late in order to get work done. Don't do either. There are better options.

How you teach people how to treat you

You teach them how to treat you by:
- how you respond to them, and
- how you approach them

As you examine your habits, you may see that you are teaching others to interrupt you at will by how you respond when they do. If you are always cordially willing to drop your current task in favor of theirs when they drop in, what have you taught them? Right! You have taught them you are always available *to them*, regardless of their subject and its priority to you or your firm.

Of course, you can also teach others NOT to bring you <u>necessary</u> information or problems by how you respond when they do. If you show irritation at them for interrupting you, they are discouraged from triggering that response again, and may avoid raising necessary issues timely just to avoid your negative reaction. So, managing interruptions requires tact, which is built in to the tactics taught here. With tactful deferrals of lower priority interruptions you don't discourage others from bringing you high-priority items.

Another way you teach people how to treat you is by how you *approach them.* For instance, if you expect *them* to allow *you to* interrupt when *you* want, they learn it is OK *to do the same to you.* Ahhh, what we do for acceptance and power!

But wait....before learning how to manage interruptions, you must believe the following statement, or no tactic to manage interruptions can be learned effectively:

"I have the right to be occasionally unavailable!"

You have the right to be unavailable during periods like these when:

- You or a family member is ill
- You are on vacation
- You are in a meeting with another client or partner
- You are preparing for a trial or important meeting with a close deadline
- You are in court

I know... good client service means being available when needed. And, of course, if there is a true emergency, you drop everything and go. Notice, however, that is not always the same as being available when *wanted*. You have a right to negotiate when to be available to the *wants* of others.

So you have precedents for YOUR RIGHT TO BE UNAVAILABLE when working on your highest priority which requires focused, concentrated time to do your best work, except for emergencies. That is when skills for understanding and managing interruptions are put to the test. So, read on to see the effects of interruptions, followed by proven tactics to manage interruptions tactfully.

The effects of interruptions

Some interruptions are beneficial; most are not.

Beneficial/Benign Interruptions:

If an interruption pertains to the priority task you are working on, then it could be very beneficial. It could be someone interrupting with a question about that task, or with information that helps your understanding of the task better or how you should handle it. No problem there, accept those.

Some self-interruptions can be helpful as well. If you are working on solving a problem, putting it aside for a while to let it 'incubate' an hour or so before coming back to it could help. For example, if you are working on arguments in support of your client's position and they don't seem very powerful, switch to another task for a while. Sometimes a good point for that argument will come to you later while you are working on another task. So, interrupt to incubate on a problem, if that works for you.

Other really short interruptions for some easy, subordinate task can be quickly handled without being too disruptive in proportion to the value of getting them out of the way. An example would be *"Hey, Jerry...could you sign this purchase order? I'd like to get it out today!"*. Stop and sign it if it is a non-controversial PO. Allow any kind of automatic task to interrupt briefly that doesn't require a lot of thought and would not be a major disruption. Accept those interruptions that keep the "wheels in motion" and remove roadblocks to others.

Of course, it is also a good habit to let your staff and associates around you know the names of individuals whom you consider to be "VIPs", meaning that no matter what you're doing you will take their call or see them if they appear in person. These individuals would be certain judges, certain attorneys, certain clients, certain family members, etc. Keep this list of names updated and communicated to others for the period in which you plan to be unavailable while working on priorities.

Harmful Interruptions:

If an interruption takes time and is not related to the top priority task you are working on, it should be resisted or managed in order to minimize its adverse impact on your concentration. For example: you are drafting a scope of work and budget estimate for your best client to be delivered to them by end of day. Mary steps into your doorway and says *"Hey,*

Jerry....Bill and I have some questions about our firm retreat next quarter, and wanted to get your input on location candidates."

The retreat is important, and you are glad to have a chance to give your input because you have some strong feelings how to improve this year's retreat and the best place to hold it. BUT...*not now, not this topic, which can wait since it is months away.* So, you would defer this one, and get right back to your client scope letter, your top priority for the moment. (You will learn how to do that at *How to use Planned, Selective Availability in* **Chapter 5. How to Manage Interruptions**)

Self-interruptions that are totally unrelated to your priority at hand, and require deep thought should be avoided. It takes discipline to stay off the web, avoid checking emails and voice mails except as planned.

Specific costs of interruptions

Keep in mind the *cost of interruptions* that require you to hop back and forth between tasks. Interruptions are costly because they:

- Stop your concentration and disrupt the nuanced associations and options you are thinking of. An important insight or action item may be totally lost, and not come to mind again after the interruption. You just can't think as deeply when distracted by interruptions.
- Take time to get focused on the new topic, and to recover from each interruption.
- Cause Loss of subtleties of thought you were engaged in. You may lose the whole train of thought!
- Irritate and stress you. The interruption itself, its subject and/or its time pressure can irritate and cause stress. You short-cut your thinking and even make mistakes that would not have been made if not irritated or stressed.

For each interruption, you must:
- Decide what, if anything, to do about/with the issue brought in by the interruption, and take necessary follow up steps before returning to the priority you were working on when interrupted.
- Retrieve the 'thread' of your thinking that leads to the 'string' that leads to the 'rope' that leads to the 'chain', and....aha! The 'gorilla' you were dealing with when interrupted comes back into focus! You have recovered by spending time to do that. One study[8] shows that interrupted information workers take an average of more than 23 minutes to get back to the original task.

Incomplete tasks due to interruptions can end up pouring over into your private time. One lawyer on the east coast said that every Sunday morning he wakes up before the rest of his family, clears off the dining room table, lays out all his casework and spends the entire Sunday just catching up on what he wasn't able to complete during the week[9]. Makes you wonder how he handles interruptions, doesn't it!

Unmanaged interruptions can create a day full of "*30-minute hours*" because of those costs. If interruptions aren't managed you'll be working more hours than necessary to get the billable work done. But by managing interruptions you'll recover a few hours each week, and be able to choose where you want to spend them.

---

8 Pattison, Kermit. "Worker Interrupted: The Cost of Task Switching." *Fast Interview.* http://www.fastcompany.com/944128/worker-interrupted-cost-task-switching., June 28,2008. February 21, 2013.
9 Ibid.

How to manage interruptions

To succeed with interruption control, you must believe that you have the *right to be unavailable sometimes*, as mentioned earlier. If you abandon this right, your work quality will suffer, and your stress will increase. The best ways to manage interruptions are:

- The Team Log
- Planned Selective Availability (PSA)
- Professional screening
- The "hideaway"

Some of these tactics are best used in combination with one or more of the others, as you will come to see as you experiment with each.

CAVEAT: Believe it or not, I've seen some autocratic partners use these techniques as a quasi-legitimate way to *avoid work*, instead of using them to help keep *themselves focused on priorities for their clients, firm and their careers*. It goes without saying that such a use is not the intent in this book.

How to use Team Logs

Before learning how to handle interruptions <u>as they occur</u>, let's examine how to use Team Logs to *prevent/head off* unnecessary interruptions by others in your firm...and even by clients!

<u>How to reduce your interruptions from your staff/matter team.</u>

Many items needing your attention that arise from your matter teams can be handled by email, text, fax or voice mail. These don't interrupt you since you are in control of when and how often you access them, and when you respond.

But, what about those interruptions *in person* by your matter team members and staff for items that <u>need to be discussed with you</u>. These don't lend themselves to electronic contact methods....they need face to face *discussion*.

Some of those interruptions may give you an opportunity to show that person who's interrupting how they could get the answer from another source, besides you. Some know how to get the answers elsewhere, but come to you simply out of their own convenience, or believing that you want them to. Reminding these individuals where to find it on their own will discourage that. Others just may not know where to find it other than coming to you, and will benefit from your showing them an alternative source for the same information.

The TEAM LOG is a good tool to cut down drastically on this type of interruption without restricting your availability or reducing good communication with your teams. Here is how it works:

- Each person on your team sets up a log with *your name*, as shown in **Figure 5** below.
- When they think of an item that needs <u>to be discussed with you</u>, they ask themself this question before interrupting you with it:

  "Can this wait?"

- If so, they write it in their log of items for you. This defers that interruption, but logs it so they won't forget it.
- If it can't wait, then they contact you to discuss. This reduces your interruptions to only those that *can't wait*.

Figure 5: Team Log Kept by Your Team Member Adam

Your Name (Adam's List)
1.Coordinate Retreat-Rachel?
2.Able corp fee reconciliation
3.Agenda for KrassCorp
meeting
4.CLE-Writing Skills-self

Over a day or two, there may be three or four more items that are deferred to their log for you.

When their log for you builds up to say five or six items, they would contact you to see when you are available to go over their *consolidated* list of _all five items_ with you in _one_ meeting instead of having interrupted you five times over that two days.

Or, if meanwhile you should contact them with something to discuss that can't wait, their five items for you can be added to the discussion after addressing your one item for them. One discussion for six items, instead of six interruptions between you two over the two days. *Defer and consolidate!*

Extreme client interruptions?

In addition to your matter team members, you may have a client or two who interrupt you a lot and would agree to defer and consolidate calls/visits to you using the same technique.

"One lawyer in Indiana told me that one client pays him about $12,000 per month to help him run his privately owned companies...relies on the lawyer for brainstorming business issues, as well as legal issues.

That client's habit was to just show up or telephone any time of day, on any day, wanting to talk. The fee income was very attractive, the legal issues were challenging and enjoyable, and counseling him on the business issues was fun. But the guy was driving this lawyer nuts with all the calls and drop-in visits whenever it struck him!

That is, until the lawyer asked and the client agreed to use a Team Log to defer and consolidate things really needing discussion, and agreed to make appointments to cover several of those items per visit or call. If no discussion was necessary, the client agreed to use email and voice mail. Problem solved, client wasn't offended, and fees continued and grew."

Your client(s) may not be this extreme, but don't overlook the possibility of negotiating the TEAM LOG approach with the *appropriate client* as well as with your matter team members.

But a better tactic for most clients is to be sure that you have provided them the names and roles of each of your associates, paralegals and secretaries working on their matter, and what aspects of the matter the client can rely on each person for if you are not available.

It helps, then, to be sure that when they visit your office, clients are introduced to each of the individuals working on their matter. This breeds trust and confidence that they can later accept information from them, rather than waiting on you.

How to reduce team and staff interruptions by you.

Similarly, here is how the TEAM LOG works for you to reduce the number of times *you interrupt* members of your team or your clients:

- Set up a log for each key team member as in **Figure 6** below. (In Word, Excel, paper, Memo app on your smart phone, etc.)
- As you think of things that <u>you need to discuss with one of them</u>, ask yourself this question before interrupting them with it:

"Can this wait?"

- <u>If it can wait</u>, write it in that person's log. This defers that interruption, but logs it so it won't be forgotten. Doing that prevents interrupting yourself and them for each item, when not absolutely, immediately necessary.
- <u>If it can't wait</u>, go ahead and contact them with your item. If they are keeping a log for you, they can bring up their deferred items to discuss at the same time.
- When you see that anyone's log accumulates to a number of items that now need discussing, set up a conversation, and use your list as the agenda. Allow them to also add any items they may have on *their log for you.*
- Should they interrupt you before your list builds to the point of scheduling a conversation with them, refer to their log sheet and cover all your accumulated

items for them at the same time you cover what they interrupted about.

- You probably already do something similar with your clients. Keeping a list of topics to discuss "when we talk next" is easy – just dumped into the file as you think of them. That way if they call you, you can cover your list in the same conversation. Or that list becomes part of your agenda for the next client meeting.

Figure 6: Team Logs That You Keep on Others

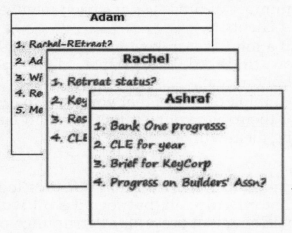

An excellent refinement to the *"Can it wait?"* question is:

"Can this wait until xx:00 o'clock XXXday for the matter team teleconference?"

If you have regular periodic matter team meetings/ telecons to take stock and monitor progress of a client's matter(s), then those become an excellent venue for raising the deferred (logged) items for discussion, especially for those items of interest to more than one team member. Plus more will get deferred when there is a time certain for dealing with them.

How to use Planned, Selective Availability

Planned, Selective Availability is the ideal mode for managing interruptions as they occur. It may be a bit more difficult than Team Logs, but it is the most productive way because someone is protecting your time.

Your system for being unavailable while working on your top priority for the moment is *professional and tactful* if it has all three of the following factors:

1. <u>Planned</u>: this implies that you have done a Written Daily Plan and are working on what is now your top-ranked priority. (See **Chapter 3: How to Benefit from a Written Daily Plan**)

2. <u>Selective</u>: this means that you will be selective and stop working on your top priority only if a higher priority item is what interrupts you. To evaluate the relative priority of the incoming interruption, these three elements must be in place:

    a. You make the *issue* be the topic and its priority, *not the person* calling/dropping in.

    b. You are willing to *defer lower priorities* rather than stop what you are doing and deal with the lower priority when it interrupts. This implies that you know the purpose, issue or reason for the interruption. You are responding to the <u>issue</u>, not to <u>the person</u> raising it.

    c. You satisfy <u>the person</u> bringing the interruption even though you don't take time to deal with it right then. Some methods to satisfy them while deferring their issue are:

        i. *Set a later time* so that you can "*…give it the time it needs…*" If the person agrees, they are satisfied with the new time to talk.

        ii. *Suggest someone else* to handle it. Again, if they agree, they are satisfied.

3. <u>Availability</u>: you will interrupt to be available for:

    a. *VIPs*: This implies that you and/or your screener have a set list of who for this day is to be a VIP. (See Appendix 5: *Professional Screening- A Script.*)

    b. *Emergencies.* This implies that you have established with your screener what qualifies as an emergency. Also communicate with your staff and clients as to what is to be considered an emergency when you are to be focused without interruption. Or, if you have no screener, you self-interrupt periodically to check voice mails to sort for emergencies that may be lurking there. You notice that PLANNED, SELECTIVE AVAILABILITY requires setting up some form of professional screening for best results.

Here is a graphic to illustrate how it works:

Figure 7: Planned, Selective Availability

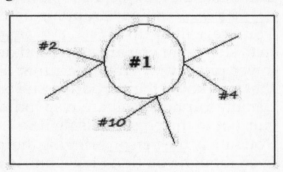

- You are working on your #1 priority for the moment, as shown in **Figure 7**. The circle represents how you protect it.
- Lower priorities (#2, #4, and #10) try for your attention (drop-in visitor or phone call).
- You defer each of them either:

  a. Yourself, by: *declining without offending* (drop-in visitor), or using voice mail, or

  b. With help from your *screener* for both drop-ins and phone calls

Hopefully, you have already overcome the temptation to assign priorities based on the medium that is bringing you the interruption: the person, phone, fax, email, messaging, etc. This confusion of "medium over message" was obvious even back in the day when faxes were first introduced. It was tempting to handle whatever came in by fax, because that "seemed important" since it arrived so quickly after it was sent to you.

Similarly, that same temptation exists today with emails, text messages, instant messages and social media tracking sites. Ignore the immediacy of the medium and focus instead on the content/subject matter and its context to determine the priority for handling/responding.

How to use professional screening

If you answer every phone call or email while working on your top priority for the moment, you are essentially giving anyone with your phone number or email address the right to set your priorities for you. But, deferring those and sticking to priorities demonstrates that you give quality time (uninterrupted) to each client matter you work on. Isn't that what clients expect?

But, can your screening really work without offending clients? Yes! When screening is properly done, you can have no fear of offending. Naturally, being available for every call would be ideal if it weren't so costly in time and concentration, and misplaced priorities. Professional Screening can be done with either:

1. A trained receptionist, or
2. You handling voice mail skillfully, or
3. You declining tactfully without offending, or
4. Any combination of the three.

A trained receptionist:

The best professional screening method is to have a PERSON do the screening. Ideally that would be a trained receptionist or administrative assistant guided by an empathic and professional script, along with some supporting arrangements, such as knowledge of your schedule, agreement on who is a VIP today, etc.

How to do that is laid out in *Appendix 5: Professional Screening-A Script*. It is a proven script for screening calls and drop-in visitors that satisfies each caller, and allows an override for VIPs and emergencies. What you do to set it up in advance is also described there for each step to work correctly.

Develop your own version of that SCRIPT to train your screener. It is <u>your</u> career, <u>you</u> train them and get their commitment to act on <u>your</u> behalf like <u>you</u> expect. Your office manager may be the one they report to, and may want some different approach, but get the screener's commitment to YOU.

A large percentage of callers will learn to rely on the professionalism of your screener when they are:
• Greeted tactfully,
• With an attitude of trying to connect them with who they want, and
• When call backs are made as promised

Screening works best when all calls are returned when promised, by *someone*. Clients <u>*expect*</u> answers, but they <u>*demand*</u> responsiveness even when an answer can't be forthcoming.

How to handle Voice Mail

The next best professional method is to have all calls go to YOUR VOICE MAIL when you are unavailable.

Properly managed, voice mail is a great interruption manager, as most professionals know. However, it has one basic flaw that disqualifies it as a client-centered tool: no priority can be assigned at the time the message is received. A message's priority can be revealed only when the message is listened to.

If you use voice mail to capture messages while you are unavailable, there are *two best practices* for managing the priorities of those messages:

BEST: Have your secretary/administrative assistant check voice mail every 15 or 30 minutes. For each message, write its details on a list for your review, capturing the following:
- Time that it came in
- Caller's name and phone number
- Subject, if left by caller
- Key message content/ details to clarify the caller's needs

The screener deletes the voice message when captured to free up your voice mail resource. The screener either handles or redirects any messages that can be handled or redirected. You are given the remaining *written list* of calls requiring your attention, along with your assistant's notes on any that have already been handled or redirected.

You quickly scan the list and evaluate the priorities, deciding to interrupt to handle or not. That quick scan interrupts you less than your having to listen to all voice mails, regardless of their priority. Instead, it is done for you, and at lower hourly cost!

SECOND BEST: You check voice mail twice in the a.m., twice in the p.m. or more or less frequently as your volume of voice mail messages requires. But, not at your every mental break out of anxiety or excessive impulse to "be available". Capture each message on a list, following the same procedure above for the screener, and trust it.

- This takes more of your time than having a screener do it, but it allows you to act on any actual emergencies, VIPs, or priority items greater than the one you are working on without taking time to interrupt for every call.
- Those messages remaining on the list can be reviewed and handled when you are done with your top priority for the moment, or delegated, or moved to your Written Daily Plan for the next day.

TIP: Create a good outgoing message (OGM).

Your OGM is what clients hear when your phone is answered automatically while you are working on your top priority for the moment. What it says is critical to maintaining your professional image and to getting the caller to leave a good message.

Here is a good example of a *30-second OGM*, followed by the rationale for each key phrase in its wording:

"Hello. This is the voice mail of (YOUR NAME). Today is Friday, February 8th. I am unavailable until 2:00 today when I will start returning calls. Please leave your name, phone number, the purpose of your call and the best time to reach you after 2:00 today. If your matter needs attention sooner, please press star 61 to speak with Stephanie Allen, my assistant. For your future calls, please feel free to press star 81 to skip this message and go directly to my voice mail."

Each key purposeful phrase in that message is described below, along with its rationale:

1. *"Hello"*. Most callers expect to hear this word when their call is answered. It is a minimum form of recognition.

2. *"This is the voice mail of (YOUR NAME)."* This sentence establishes two things:

   a. That the caller has reached a voice mail. Some OGM recordings are of such high fidelity it sounds like a live person is answering, so this clarifies that it is not.

   b. That they have reached *your* voice mail. If that's what they intended, they will relax and listen on. If that's NOT what they intended, they can hang up.

3. *"Today is Friday, February 8th."* Stating the date shows that you are up to date, a mark of diligence and attention. It implies that you are checking messages at least daily when you update the OGM. Hearing the correct date makes your OGM credible, unlike the impression given by a generic message.

4. *" I am unavailable until 2:00 today when I will start returning calls."* I know…this sentence is not one you probably now include. Yes, it implies that you intend to return the call, and gives a possible time you'll do it. Giving a time for callbacks is a big help to the caller as to whether to leave the message, or to call your assistant.

   Of course, if 2:00 the same day is not workable, at least give them an indication of when to expect the call back. *"I'll return your call by the end of the day tomorrow,"* if that is what you intend. The point is, if you can state your intentions, your caller with have more trust in the fact that you will call back. If call backs are not made timely, your screening system loses its

47

professionalism and credibility. Failure to return calls timely is one of the most frequent complaints about lawyers.

5. *"Please leave your name, phone number, the purpose of your call and the best time to reach you after 2:00 today."* This specific list of information to leave increases the likelihood that they will comply.

If they leave you the best time to reach them within the callback period you have given in your OGM, you can at least try to call them then. Let's say the caller says "*...the best time to reach me after 2:00 is 3:00-3:30... .*". Great! If you can call them back within 3:00-3:30, you'll likely catch them available and avoid 'phone tag'. Plus, if they are not available, you have their implied permission to tell their screener that you are "*...returning Mr. Keller's phone call request for 3:15...*".

If you have a client or opposing attorney who objects to leaving their number because "*...you already know my number...*" just explain that leaving it with their message expedites the call back: you save the time of looking it up if you return the call, and if your assistant routes it appropriately to someone else on the team to return, they have the number right in the message.

Occasionally, you may have a client reluctant to leave the topic or reason for their call because of their 'confidentiality' concerns, or privacy sensitivity. That is understandable in some cases. However, if you have properly credentialized your staff with your clients, callers will trust that your staff adheres to the same ethics rules of confidentiality that you must follow as a lawyer, and be more likely to leave details in their message.

If you don't get the reason/topic/issue for their call, you won't know how to set your priority for the call back, unless they are a VIP, or unless there is only one topic they ever call about.

6. *" If your matter needs attention sooner, please press star 61 to speak with Stephanie Allen, my assistant."* CAUTION: Be sure Stephanie will be there, will answer and that you are not sending them to another voice mail. Callers hate being sent to that type of 'voice jail'.
   Again, this works best if you have informed your clients of Stephanie's qualifications...who she is, what her job is, and her qualifications. If clients know that you trust her completely to be up to date on client matters administratively and on finding you when needed, then her involvement is seen to be good client service and a professional way to handle calls without having to wait for your availability.

7. *"For your future calls, please feel free to press star 81 to skip this message and go directly to my voice mail"* This sentence is for your frequent callers. If they know how to skip your 30-second OGM, they can immediately do so, and not have to listen to it for the umpteenth time. Providing them a way to skip your 30-second OGM is considerate of their time, and will be appreciated. That is one more subtle way your screening is professional and client centered.

How to handle email

The good news about email is that an audio and/or visual alert from your computer or smart phone can be set to tell you when a new email arrives. That way you don't have to continually keep your inbox screen within view.

The bad news about email is that the alert/pop-up is triggered for *every* email. I'm unaware of any device that can be set to indicate the incoming message's priority by a different sound for a different source or topic, in the same way that your smart phone can attach identifying ringer sounds to incoming calls by person. Happily, you can turn off the alerts and use some of the tips below instead.

Here are some tips for saving time in managing emails:

1. Turn off the sound/pop-up alerts on your devices when you need to focus on your number one priority for the moment.

2. Have your secretary or admin periodically throughout the day screen and filter your emails, identifying those that require interrupting you, need action by you later or can be redirected to someone else.

3. If having emails screened is not available to you, then set a reminder on your smart phone to check emails every hour or half hour. That's better than being interrupted every time a new one comes in.

4. For internal emails, get your colleagues to agree to always attach the message thread to save you time from having to look up the prior message details to which they refer.

5. Try to get your clients and colleagues (and yourself!) to use meaningful subject lines that reflect the true content of the message, and maybe even its urgency.

6. Get clients to agree to use email only for FYI-type messages. Have them use the phone or appointments for things that are urgent or need discussing. Encourage them to request a phone appointment or an in-person appointment.

7. Get the partners, associates and staff with whom you work most frequently to agree not to send by email those requests for action or task assignments that are time sensitive. Those are handled better by conversation anyway. But removing them from email traffic reduces your feeling of possibly "missing an important email" when working on a priority.

8. Master your email settings for routing frequent offender spam to the spam folder. That way you do not have to confront them as they come in. You can then review spam and delete them weekly or monthly, instead of having to respond to them daily.

How to decline tactfully without offending

For those low priority drop-in interruptions or calls that get by your voice mail and your screener, you must fall back on PLANNED, SELECTIVE AVAILABILITY and defer those _yourself._ That requires knowing how to saying "No" to their request on the spot without offending. The key sequential five steps for saying "No" (i.e., declining a request) without offending are as follows, followed by a full description of each:

1. Acknowledge their request and its importance to them.
2. Decline without using negative words.
3. Give your reasons for declining...as specifically as you can.
4. Suggest alternative ways they can get what they need.
5. Negotiate.

Here's an example of how to do that, and the model script for those five key steps.

Example: You are working on your top priority for the moment, and Dudley, another lawyer in your practice group, pops in and says:

"Hey...could you take just a few minutes to help me work out the agenda for a meeting I'm having at 1:30 tomorrow afternoon with a client and his insurance adjuster? The insurance company is taking their usual hard position like "...what fire?..." and I need some ideas on how to keep the agenda focused on our basis for calculating the loss and *avoid all the manipulative side issues the adjuster will try to introduce."*

Your response using the five steps:

1. <u>Acknowledge the request's importance to the person asking.</u>

   "I can see that will be an important meeting for setting the negotiating tone, for sure."

   This acknowledges the *importance <u>to Dudley</u>,* even though it is not <u>*equally important to you*</u>. By saying it like this, Dudley 'gets it' that you not only <u>heard</u> him, but that *it is ok that he asked you.* He feels <u>validated</u> with your understanding the importance of this meeting to him and his client.

   Don't skip this *acknowledgement* step and instead go right to the next step, *declining.* That is a common mistake that causes a missed opportunity to establish rapport with Dudley before declining. When Dudley knows he's been heard, he is more likely to listen to you. So *acknowledge his need!*

2. <u>Decline to deal with it right now, if ever.</u>

   "My situation is…", or *"My problem is…*

   This reference to your "situation" or "problem" alerts Dudley that you are about to *describe the barrier* that prevents you from to saying "yes" to his request.

3. <u>Give your reason.</u>

   " My situation/problem is that… I must get this scope and budget completed for Aamalgamite Inc. and it will take me the rest of the day. It has to go out tonight."

   When you offer your <u>specific reason</u>, it clarifies your situation, and builds trust. *Not offering a reason* risks appearing to reject Dudley arbitrarily and personally.

Giving a reason establishes that you are 'reasonable' (able to reason), even if Dudley doesn't agree with its importance. Your reason is important to you, and that is what you are establishing clearly.

So, with steps 2 & 3 you have clearly declined by describing an explicit barrier stated directly with no equivocation.....your decline is complete, and it is clear to Dudley that you won't be interrupting to help him right now. But, you declined without ever using *any* negative words/syllables like, "*...no, not...n't.... im-....un-....etc.*"

4. Offer alternatives to meet Dudley's needs.

I could spend some time with you on it tomorrow morning just before noon. Or, if not, maybe you could check with Warwick Higgins....he's really good at dealing with insurance adjusters!

If you *never* wanted to help Dudley on this issue, you could leave out the offer to help tomorrow morning, and go with only the reference to Higgins. In any case, offering an alternative or two to what Dudley is requesting is a gesture of your good faith, whether or not either alternative involves you. It shows that you are *interested in Dudley getting his needs met*, even as you decline to do it right now.

Failing to offer alternative solutions would be seen as indifference to Dudley's needs. Taking time to think of a couple of alternatives is an investment in your relationship with Dudley, and requires less of your time than doing what he asked.

5. Negotiate.

No doubt Dudley will likely not just accept your response and walk away. It is more likely that he will offer some argument to get you to reconsider.

Dudley says: *"But, this would take only 10-15 minutes of your time, I'm sure. And we've got a $12million settlement at stake here....is your Amalgamite case really more important than that? "*

By 'negotiate' is meant to listen to Dudley's further push to get your agreement, and respond to it with reason while standing your ground if Dudley's argument doesn't change your mind.

You say:

"It's not a matter of what's most at stake, Dudley. It is a matter of keeping my commitment to the Amalgamite GC to get this matter budget to him so he can get a place holder for our fees in their next quarter's budget. If I spent time with you now, I would have to work late to do that, and I have commitments after work. Sorry!

By taking a moment to exchange a point or two of argument, instead of giving him an ultimatum (which would have been quicker) you have invested a little in your relationship with Dudley. After all, how you handle Dudley's request can affect how he handles your next request for help from him.

And, even if <u>he persuaded you to change your initial position</u> and you agree to take the *"...15 minutes..."*, your method of initially declining has benefitted you in that Dudley would know what <u>you had to overcome</u> to help him (working late, breaking your after-work commitment, etc.). Doing <u>all that would increase the value of your accommodation</u>. But, if you had agreed initially, saying nothing about your Amalgamite commitment, working late, or your after-work commitment, it might have seemed to Dudley that you were just looking for an interesting interruption like his.

Remember: *we teach people how to treat us by how we respond to them!*

Happily, this script for declining without offending can be used *for personal or professional times when you are asked to do something that you can't do or don't want to do.* It is intended for use when the person asking is one with whom you want to maintain a positive relationship. Those five steps are intended to avoid the appearance of indifference to the person requesting, while getting your own needs met without doing so at the expense of the person asking.

It is easier to agree sometime just to keep a relationship 'positive' and without tension, especially if we don't know how to get our own needs met without offending the other party. Sure, it may seem easier to agree than to risk the conflict involved in tactfully declining…no one likes to "pet the porcupine".

But, this script builds in wording that respects the needs of the one requesting, without agreeing to what they want. If you practice and learn this script you'll have the ability to decline when you must without offending the relationship… at work, at home, in community affairs, etc.

Of course, if the relationship with the person asking you is of little or no ongoing importance to you, then you can decline any way you want, including "no thanks….I'm just not interested"…like when you get the phone call at home asking for a donation to some cause that doesn't interest you.

How to Use a Hideaway

The Hideaway method is a crude, less structured way of exercising your right to be temporarily unavailable, but without some of the advantages of the PLANNED, SELECTIVE AVAILABILITY method above.

As it suggests, you achieve protection from interruptions by "hiding away" from your office. Go to your library, or another vacant office, Starbucks or any place where you can concentrate on your main priority for the moment away from the usual hubbub of your office. When others don't know where you are, they can't interrupt you!

Of course, if you hide away, at least one person on your team...secretary, receptionist, or colleague...should know where you are in case of true emergencies. When anyone asks for you during this period, they are simply told "... *(Your name) is out of the office until...*" whatever time you plan to return. If they can leave a message, all the better.

There is less risk of this unavailability tactic if you have a qualified screener handling your visitors, voice mail, and email while you are "hiding away". If voice mails and emails are not checked during your hide away time, the risk is that a hot one could come in right at the beginning of your hide-away period, and worsen before you check voice mail on your return.

✂ ✂ ✂

Chapter 6

How to Improve Daily Time Keeping

It is virtually impossible to analyze how to improve your time management and personal organization without an accurate, specific record of where your time is actually going now. So, record your time, at least daily, if not contemporaneously after each task.... including the unbillable hours periodically (more on unbillable hours in a moment).

Most lawyers would just as soon put off _daily timekeeping_. After all, it can be a painstaking chore. It seems at first to be simply a "housekeeping" task rather than actual legal work. I've actually heard otherwise brilliant lawyers say something like this:

"I went to school to become a lawyer, not a data entry clerk!"

But, not recording time daily can deprive you of the information you need to bill properly and to analyze your time management effectiveness. Plus, putting off recording your time can end up causing difficulties, such as lost revenue, fee disputes, or ethics complaints.

How daily entries help avoid lost revenue

If you wait until the end of the day, week or (even worse) the end of the month, to record that period's time, it is more than likely that you will not remember all legitimate time charged and/or the correct duration of those tasks because memories fade. This "shrinkage" (Hours worked minus hours recorded= shrinkage) takes a toll on billable hours, already at risk for write-downs and past due accounts receivable, as shown in **Figure 8**.

Figure 8: How Revenue Shrinks from Hours Worked

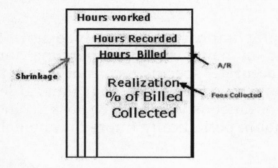

An ideal habit is to document your time immediately after a client task is completed. Doing that avoids the shrinkage likely if you try to re-create the file at the end of the day, week or month.

How daily entries help avoid fee disputes

It's likely that much of your work on a client matter will be done out of the client's view so they can't observe you doing it. Also, it's likely that your client doesn't have a clear picture of all the steps it takes to achieve what you've promised to deliver. After all, they came to you because of your superior (to them) knowledge of legal processes. So the time records are educational for them to see exactly what work you do.

Since law is not a science, there will be times where you can't get the outcome that the client wants. But you did the work. Accurate and detailed time records show what work you did on their behalf in pursuit of an outcome that could not be guaranteed. So capture your time daily, if not contemporaneously.

How daily Time entries help avoid ethics complaints

As you no doubt know, fee disputes or questions are one of the greatest sources of grievances against attorneys. So, anything you can do to clarify the legitimate details of your work will help the client understand what was required to serve them as agreed. And should a disgruntled client file a legal malpractice claim, one of the first things the former client's new counsel requests is a copy of your time records. Itemized records show exactly what work you performed when each task shown starts with a verb (draft…, research…, interview…, etc.)

How to get five additional benefits of daily time entries

Here are some other reasons that it pays off to record your time immediately, specifically and directly into your billing system:

1. **Frees up staff time:** Some lawyers still insist on writing their time entries on a form or legal pad and giving it to the secretary for entering into the timekeeping system. Those lawyers could just as quickly enter those details themselves directly into the firm's timekeeping system as they occurred. That would save the secretary hours per week for more productive work.

2. **Clarifies your work for clients.** Time records allow your firm to produce itemized bills that educate clients about the legal process and show the time and effort you have spent, assuring them that you are working on their behalf.

3. **Protects firm profitability.** For hourly matters, trying to re-create a file at the end of the week or month will cause errors. It is more likely you will undercharge than overcharge. For contingency or flat fee matters, knowing your exact hourly investment will help keep your eye on the profitability of that work, and whether it is as good as you expect.

4. **Helps analyze your productivity.** Your goal should be to bill a higher percent of the hours you actually spend in the office, and at a higher realization percentage. The best way to monitor that is to have a clear record of where every hour of your day goes. Your time system will be a pretty good record of your billable time, but you need other administrative codes to capture the nonbillable time for analysis. (See *Appendix 1: How To Take and Analyze a Time Log*)

5. **Shows where nonbillable time went.** Most legal timekeeping systems focus almost exclusively on allowing you to record only *your billable time*. But, until you know where *your nonbillable time is going*, there is little hope that you will be able to address any bad habits in time management that you may have.

   Your firm no doubt has some administrative time codes allowing capture of activities like business development activity, research, training of staff, and your own continuing legal education. But the more admin codes you have the better to capture most of your non-billable time. That's where the bad habits will reveal themselves and probably be relatively easy to correct. Remember: *"A well stated problem is half solved."*

Having both billable and nonbillable time available in detail is the secret to getting an accurate measure of your productivity, and where it could improve, if needed.

You wouldn't want to log unbillable time every day; it is best recorded only periodically. Select a short period, say, only two or three days per month. For those days, record ALL unbillable time, and analyze it at the end of the period. The key question to ask, as you analyze these unbillable time records is: *"What took my time and contributed little or prevented my working effectively on priorities?"* When you have identified the inefficiencies, you can begin selecting tactics from this book that might help.

Putting off recording your time erodes all the above benefits of contemporaneous timekeeping.

However, keep in mind that *recording your time* is not the same as *billing it*. You can't bill it, if it's not recorded. But, if you record it and then decide *not to bill* some of it, the cost of not billing it is easily calculated. You can't analyze it if it's not recorded.

You can't calculate utilization percentage and the effect of write-downs if it's not recorded. That's why it is a "sin to eat time", meaning don't perform work without recording it to the client matter just because you're not sure if it can be billed. Make that decision when you bill, not when you do the work.

✄ ✄ ✄

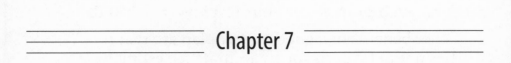

Chapter 7

How to Improve Matter Management

Well-planned legal matters save time by helping you to avoid tense conversations with clients re: fee surprises, and reduces the time you'll spend delegating the associated tasks and monitoring work done by others on the matter team.

Immediately upon being awarded new work, either verify the matter plan and budget included in the proposal, or craft one immediately if it has not already been done. It can cost unnecessary time if you wait to the last minute to begin working on the matter plan instead of planning it out at proposal time or immediately upon receiving the work.

That's because a surprise late in a matter's life may require a complex solution that cannot be developed with high quality under time pressure. The later a plan is developed in the life of a matter, the more response capability is lost.

How good matter planning and budgeting helps

Drafting a matter plan immediately after receiving the new matter protects your response capability with more time to overcome any surprises and still complete the balance of work on time. That is one benefit of doing a detailed matter plan (a *Work Breakdown Schedule* in current Legal Project Management[10] terms) *as soon as possible* after you agree to take on each matter. Of course, some matter plans are done in an advance of receiving the work in order to estimate a fee for a pitch proposal or your response to an RFP.

Other benefits of a good matter plan are that it:
- Provides a basis for an accurate fee estimate.
- Identifies the tasks required, allowing them to be delegated and scheduled.
- Identifies the other individuals needed to complete the work early enough to ensure they will be available when needed.
- Increases the likelihood that the work will be accomplished *on time* without getting sidetracked or interrupted. (For additional important benefits of early matter planning, see *Appendix 6: Key Benefits of Matter Planning.*)

Doing a matter plan is a good way to begin work on a case. Beginning work sets in motion the Zeigarnik effect: *the tendency to experience intrusive thoughts about an objective that was started but not finished* [11].

That is why interruptions that cause you to fall behind on the work also cause anxiety that brings about constant thoughts of that unfinished business[12].

So, in effect, starting work on a matter with a plan creates a tendency to keep it top of mind until it is

---

10 For a definitive understanding of what is involved in Legal Project Management, see Hassett, Jim,Ph.D, *Legal Project Management Quick Reference Guide,* 3rd Edition, 2013, LegalBizDev.

11 Baumeister, he, R.F., & Bushman, B.J., (2008). Social Psychology and Human Nature. United States: Thompson Wadsworth p. 122.

12 Johnson, P.B., Mehrabian, A., Weiner, B. (1968). Achievement Motivation and the Recall of Incompleted and Completed Exam Questions. Journal of Educational Psychology, 59(3), 181-185.

finished and to protect it from interruption. That is another reason to involve team members in creating the matter plan so that they too experience this same helpful need to complete it.

How to write a task level matter plan/budget

<u>One approach to writing a matter plan</u> and estimating the fee budget is to analyze past similar matters your firm has worked on. That works if the past matter was done well and efficiently. But if not, its errors will be imported into the new plan. Also, it can be quite a tedious, time-consuming job, unless time entries for the past matter are coded with discrete task codes. Even with good codes, most time records are not easy to analyze in terms of a new matter at hand.

When you are experienced with similar matters, it is best to use your own imagination and recollections to identify the best steps for the <u>_new matter at hand,_</u> drawing on your past experience and the matters unique requirements. Trust yourself to envision the work tasks that are likely to be involved, and describe them as tasks in the work plan.

<u>Another approach is used when you haven't recently or have never handled a similar matter</u>. Talk with those who have, listen to ideas on what worked well and what should be done differently. Then give it your best shot.

But if there is no one who has had experience and there are no past similar matters, then use your imagination by envisioning the steps you can foresee, as though you are watching a video of the work being done from beginning to end, capturing each envisioned task description in writing.

A good template for doing a matter plan would look something like this:

Figure 9: Matter Planning Template

Task/ Activity	Who	Est. # Hours	$ Hrly Rate	$ Fee Est.	Due By

Done in a Word table or an Excel worksheet allows sorting by phase or in appropriate sequence after listing all the tasks and the information in its row.

Steps for creating a matter plan

1. <u>List each required task *as you think of them*</u>, in the order that you think they should be done. Each task has a beginning, an amount of time needed to complete it and an ending.

   The interdependent tasks can be resorted into their proper sequence once all tasks are identified and listed.

   <u>The greater the number of tasks, and the smaller the tasks</u>, the more accurate your budget estimate will be. That's because estimating errors are smaller as a percentage of the total time for smaller tasks than for larger tasks, resulting in a more accurate aggregate estimate of time. Don't let yourself fall for the erroneous belief that keeping the scope *more general* leaves you

"more room to move." Recognize that, instead, keeping it *general* increases the probability that there will be disputes on what was originally included in the first place. Specifics and detail clarify and clarity breeds trust.

Henry Ford said it this way: *"Nothing is particularly hard if you divide it into small jobs."*

2. <u>Begin each task with an action word (verb)</u>....*find, calculate, call, draft,* etc. The verb you use helps establishes the beginning and ending of the task. For example, *draft* the agreement is a discrete task different from *signing* the agreement.

   Be sure that you, the client, and the matter team assign the same meaning to the **action words**. It is very helpful to write up a glossary of commonly used ones to establish their meanings. Examples:

   - *Ascertain:* find out with certainty
   - *Consider:* think about; decide
   - *Create:* cause to be; make
   - *Establish:* set up; settle; prove beyond dispute
   - *Formulate:* put together; add; express
   - *Inspect:* examine carefully or officially
   - *Observe:* inspect; watch
   - *Plan:* devise a scheme for doing; make or arrange activities to achieve objectives

   Clear action words help establish the beginning and ending for a task, and determine the duration of the task.

3. <u>Leave line space between each task</u> written to accommodate tasks you think of later that should be inserted earlier in the task sequence. This will allow you to benefit from your insights on proper sequencing of the work as your thinking gets more involved in details of the matter.

4. <u>Don't number the tasks</u> in order until you are done listing them. When you review the finished list, you'll begin to sense the interdependency of which tasks must be completed before other tasks can begin. Of course, some tasks can be performed in parallel, i.e. at the same time, which is good for efficiency.

5. <u>Estimate the time required to accomplish *each* task</u>, if it could be done efficiently, and without interruption (its incurred time). This estimate is for *fee calculation purposes*, and not for planning the timeline or *duration* of the task. The duration of a task will be governed by available staff, and the degree to which other tasks must be completed first.

6. <u>Identify the responsible party</u> (or staff rank) for each task, if not to be done by you.

   Be careful not to "over-lawyer" the matter, meaning don't assign more individuals to work on this matter than are absolutely needed. You'll automatically consider staffing some of the work at the lowest level possible, i.e., where the information and judgment exist that are required for quality work.

   However, don't overlook the possibility of delegating "up" in rank to an experienced lawyer with higher rates, but who could do it so much more quickly that the ultimate total fee would be less than delegating those tasks "down" or doing them yourself.

7. <u>Place due dates on the tasks</u> that require completion in order to meet your ultimate deadline. Enter these in your calendar, and use them to monitor progress of the work. (**See Chapter 8: How to Delegate Effectively** for tips on how to set these due dates and deadlines.)

8. <u>Total the time required</u> for all tasks to get an estimate of incurred time (billable time) for the matter/phase.

9. <u>Write up the assumptions</u> and carve-outs on which the plan is based. Once you have the entire task list in front of you, you can infer the assumptions that were tacitly guiding your list, plus you will think of other assumptions and carve-outs that need to be identified. You'll want to state these in your Scope of Work section of your engagement letter.

10. <u>Think of what might go wrong</u> (possible risks) during work on this matter plan. Decide how likely each risk is to occur, and estimate how significant would be the impact if it did occur. Those risks with high likelihood and significant impact merit further planning discussion as to how to mitigate or avoid their damage to the matter plan and budget should they occur.

The relatively little amount of time it takes to discuss these high probability, high-impact risks (the "ounce of prevention") can save a lot of time (the "pound of cure") that would be required to handle a risk if it arises without forethought.

Additional Tips to consider

When creating a matter plan using the steps above, consider these tips:

- If it is a huge matter that will obviously require work over many months, consider estimating in phases, with the most detailed task breakout for the earliest phase. The further out you plan, the less likely it is that the plan will be realistic. Winston Churchill put it this way:

  "It is a mistake to look too far ahead. Only one link of the chain of destiny can be handled at a time."

- Develop the matter plan through discussion with all members of your matter team instead of doing it alone.
- In fact, consider whether the team should draft the initial matter plan themselves and submit it for your review and approval.
- Have whoever will be doing a task make the initial estimate of how much time that task will take. The person who will be doing the work will usually give the best estimate of how much time they will require. Then, if you or the team disagrees, the estimate can be improved by discussion and your final decision.

When team members *participate* in creating a matter plan, *a sense of ownership* is created among them and therefore they *will be more committed* to its success.

Anatomy of a client matter

A good way to summarize the whole of matter planning is to look at what happens structurally in every matter from beginning to end. Every matter has the same fundamental elements. How well each element is managed determines client satisfaction, realization, efficiency and profit.

Naming each of these elements assists in focusing on how robustly each element is managed during work on a matter. For example, depending upon how well and how early the work for a matter is planned, the "steps" or "tasks" generally get accomplished whether planned in advance or not, accomplished in an effective order or not and done with the right people or not.

The most common dysfunctions I have encountered center around either trying to plan too far into the future, or not specifically enough. A third runner-up problem is ineffective progress checking: accomplishments versus plan. When progress is checked along the way, deadlines are less likely to slip. When progress is not checked along the way, communication internally and with the client can be affected adversely and deadlines are at risk.

The image in **Figure 10** is an 'X-Ray' view of any matter, showing its 'anatomy'. Each numbered part is explained below the figure.

Figure 10: Anatomy of a Matter

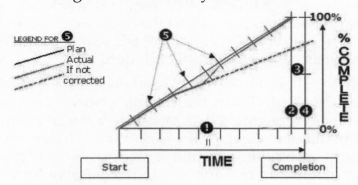

❶Tasks required to complete the work over time. It is best to plan the work as soon as possible after it has been awarded. That way all tasks can be seen at once before beginning. Each task has a beginning and an ending, and requires time to accomplish. A good matter budget/fee estimate requires a realistic statement of each task.

❷Target Date, when work would be completed if all goes as planned (usually quite unlikely – Murphy's laws have not been repealed, to my knowledge!). But if the target date is actually met, then you have successfully "under-promised and over-delivered", a good habit for client relationships. I've never heard of a client complaining about work being finished ahead of schedule!

❸Contingency, to allow for surprises and underesti- mates. Promise the client to deliver by the 'Deadline' but you and the matter team will try to complete it by the 'Target Date'. A contingency gives you room to 'wiggle' without a change order for minor surprises in underestimation, assumptions and carve-outs.

(CAUTION: Don't hide the true deadline from the matter team by claiming that the target date is the deadline. That usually breeds hostility, especially when a legitimate delay requires work beyond the target date. Explaining at that time that "we're O.K.... .I left a little cushion I didn't tell you about...."will be seen as having manipulated them.)

❹Deadline: Initial promise date. (See the discussion of DEADLINES in the section below). The deadline can be renegotiated if tasks are required outside of the initial budget, or if assumptions change, or carve- outs become impossible to exclude. Usually, howev- er, clients do not appreciate *this pushing back of dead- lines.* That puts a premium on step 5 below: Progress Checks.

❺Progress Checks: Done regularly to compare actual progress of work completed vs. work planned. If ac- tual completed work matches the plan at a progress check, all is well. But if not, the questions are *"How can we get back on track by next progress check ?"* or *"... Can we afford to renegotiate the deadline?"*

Target dates and progress checks are the elements in man- aging legal work that are most often under managed by the matter team leader. Better attention to these two elements can greatly enhance the morale of your team, improve client satisfaction, and reduce your stress.

If progress checks are not robustly conducted, things can easily fall behind schedule and absorb any contingency that could have been preserved by earlier action when work first fell behind.

Don't confuse duration with incurred time

A new matter cannot always be started immediately, even if it is already planned. That's because you may need to work on other near-term deadlines for matters in progress already. But apart from that scenario, the usual main reason for starting late is confusing the *duration* or *life* of a matter with the *incurred/chargeable time* required to complete all its tasks.

For example, say it is the 1st day of the month when you get the go ahead for some work from your good client, Smith. It could be tempting to think like this:

"This Smith matter will take only 25-30 hours and they don't need it until the end of next month. Since I have 60 days to complete it, I'll start work on it in a couple of weeks."

The figure below helps think about how work can be ideally distributed over the duration of a matter from day 1 to its completion.

Figure 11: Duration and Incurred Times

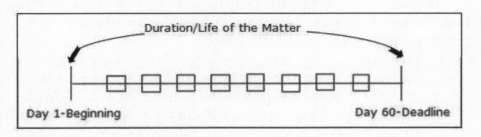

The boxes represent the 30 hours of work distributed as it will most likely be incurred during work periods on Smith over its two month life. Smith is probably not your only open matter in process or that will arise during the 60 days, so the Smith work sessions would be interspersed among work sessions on those other matters. Few lawyers have the good fortune of being able to work on only one case at a time from beginning to end.

The temptation to put off starting in earnest on Smith can be reinforced by these circumstances:

- You have other matters in progress, some with earlier deadlines. Deciding to finish those before starting Smith is tempting, and appropriate in some situations.

- You may feel that you work better under pressure, so waiting until closer to the deadline will provide you the needed pressure. The problem is, the pressure will be there causing you to risk oversights, make mistakes and do less than high-quality work.

- You may confuse the "60 days until due" by thinking instead *"I have 60 days available, but the Smith matter requires only 30 hours…no sweat!"* But, that is not a rational comparison because it fails to account for the work you must do on other matters during that same 60 days.

Any delay before beginning work on Smith reduces your response capability to deal with surprises from unexpected additional work on Smith, health problems or emergencies from other clients, etc. For example, compare these two extreme scenarios for the Smith case:

1. <u>You start by planning the second day</u> after receiving the work, even though it is 60 days until you have to deliver finished product. You begin work on the eighth day. Then, on the 10th day you discover a major surprise in the opposing counsel's strategy. You

now have a *good 50 days* to overcome the surprise and complete the work.

-OR-

2. You start by planning on the 40<u>th</u> day after receiving the work, now that three other projects are behind you. You begin work on the 46th day. That leaves 14 days to complete the 30 hours, or a little over two hours per day required. Then, on the 48th day you discover a major surprise in the opposing counsel's strategy. You now have *12 days* to overcome the surprise <u>and</u> complete the work.

Which is better: 50 days to overcome the surprise and complete the work or 12 days to overcome the surprise and complete the work?

How to avoid scope creep: the "Reality Triangle"

Scope creep is when the original task list expands during work on a legal matter, largely as a result of the lawyer and the team either granting client change requests or discovering and doing needed work not foreseen in the original scope.

To guard against scope creep, it's important to identify and manage the trade-offs needed among three key elements (scope, resources and timing), so that they remain optimized during the conduct of the matter, as shown in **Figure 12** below.

In an accurate matter plan, the relationship of these three key elements is established like this:
• The scope/tasks involved (with the assumptions and carve outs) determine what resources are needed in order to complete those tasks. "Resources" refer to required lawyer and staff hours, software, outside services like jury consultants, etc.

- When resources are identified, the fee and the deadline or delivery date can be estimated fairly accurately for that planned list of tasks. For example, if you are short staffed, it may take longer to complete the work than if not short staffed.

Once those three factors-scope, resources/fee and schedule- are optimized, that becomes the plan against which progress should be monitored and managed. Then, after beginning the work, if a surprise occurs in any one of those factors, *an adjustment must be made in at least one of the three factors* to accommodate the surprise optimally.

For example, if midway through the matter the client decides the work must be completed sooner in order to present results at an emergency board meeting, either the fee will need to increase, or some of the tasks will need to be done differently or dropped, or both. If neither is acceptable to the client, maybe you can't agree to deliver for the emergency board meeting! Such trade-offs are required to re-optimize this closed system.

That is why I call the interrelationship of these three elements the "Reality Triangle" – it is the reality of every legal matter.

Figure 12: The "Reality" Triangle

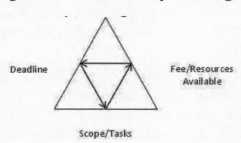

Understanding this closed system means that when surprises or client requests require work outside the scope, you *must be willing to refer to the matter plan and identify the neces-sary trade-offs* to be communicated to the client, so they are involved in the decision as to how to proceed.

How to use change orders

If accommodating a scope change or other type of surprise involves a change in deadline or an increase in fee, the best practice is to get a *change order* signed by the client. Change orders, properly managed, save a lot of time that otherwise would be wasted in confusion, misunderstanding and strained client relationships over "fee surprises".

When you go to a client to request a change order, be pre-pared to provide the client the following information:
- The reason the added work is needed
- The reason the added work was not anticipated in the original work plan.
- The benefit to the client of doing the work
- The harm to the client if the added work is not done
- Possible trade-offs in scope fee and timing to consider
- Circumstances under which you will stop work if no change order is approved. Rarely needed, but one must be willing to "stop the bleeding" when the fees at stake are substantial enough to do so.

Tip: if your practice doesn't already have one, it's rec-ommended that you write up a "change order procedure". Then, in your engagement letter, a section of it can describe how change orders will be administered. By "pre-calling" the existence and possible need for a change order at the beginning of the matter, it will be less of a surprise, and eas-ier to implement should the need for one arise. The written change order procedure can include details like how many out-of-scope hours or dollars would trigger a change order, and how small changes would be aggregated in order to avoid the sensation of "nickel-diming" the client with repeated small adjustments.

Notice the presumption throughout the above comments that the original scope is sufficiently detailed. Without a detailed task breakdown in your scope, it's virtually impossible to demonstrate to the client that the new work was absent from that original scope, and therefore requires some change in other parts of the scope, fee or timing in order to re-optimize the work plan.

How to use deadlines and 'Time Activating'

*"A task without a deadline is a dream.
And dreams die easily."*

(Spoken to the author by the late Dr. R. Alec MacKenzie, author of <u>The Time Trap</u> and co-author of <u>It's About Time</u>).

Most lawyers I've met consider the word "deadline" to refer to some external requirement imposed by the client, the court, a contract, lien, etc. Other less formal synonyms are: *due date, end date, drop-dead date,* or *target date.* However, the following preferable definition of the word "deadline" covers the main meaning in all of those terms:

The deadline is the 'line' over which if you step you are 'dead' in some way.

In other words, it's the point in time *after which point you and/or your client are uncomfortable if the task or matter in question isn't finished.*

"Uncomfortable" refers to the fact that past that point, there is some:
• Penalty,
• Disadvantage,
• Loss of value in the work already done, or

- Some sort of disappointment

Good client relationships demand that deadlines are clear to avoid client discomfort. And remember: deadlines are a time promise, regardless of the substantive nature of the content. Whether it pertains to a really important issue, or a trivial one, the deadline is still an expectation. So, meet it or negotiate changing it, but never miss it.

"Time activating" is another helpful habit related to deadlines. Time activating is when you place a 'deadline' on yourself, even when there is no external deadline, such as a client promise, court date, filing deadline, etc.

Deadlines and time activated tasks create an appropriate sense of urgency that helps you get work done efficiently, on time and under budget. They help keep you focused and resistant to sidetracks and interruptions. That's why deadlines are a good time management habit.

> Client or Partner: *"Thanks, Amanda. Just do it as soon as you can, please."*

> Amanda: *"You're welcome, Marty. I'll get right on it!!"*

What just happened in that conversation? No clear expectation as to delivery date was established, that's for sure! It will be difficult for Amanda to meet Marty's expectation since she doesn't know exactly what it is.

This type of exchange happens all too often in trusting relationships. Other common, similarly dysfunctional, phrases are "early next week" or "as soon as possible".

Marty resisted giving Amanda a deadline, probably because he did not want to seem pushy. Amanda wanted to show urgency, but without detail. She may, in fact, have felt some relief that Marty didn't give her a specific deadline. She intends to move it forward 'quickly', and trusts that will satisfy Marty. *The problem is that Marty will probably be looking for it earlier than Amanda plans to deliver it.*

This is a good opportunity for Amanda to clarify their agreement as to *when* the work is to be completed. Doing so saves time by avoiding time-consuming conversations and disputes over missed expectations that were never defined in the first place.

Since Marty wasn't specific, what should Amanda have done? She could have probed for Marty's true preference by asking:

"When would you ideally like to have this back in your hands, Marty?"

If Marty remained non-committal (*"Oh, just as soon as you can..."*), Amanda could have taken a moment to review her calendar and respond with a specific delivery time that works for her with a liberal margin for error, such as:

"... How would Wednesday at 3:00 be, Marty?"

In any case, it is better to have agreed upon a mutually acceptable delivery time, rather than leaving it undefined and subject to misunderstanding.

In summary, the main benefits of deadlines are that they:

1. Provide visible evidence of competence, when set and met
2. Allow comparison of expectation vs. actual results
3. Energize task focus
4. Enhance communication
5. Clarify the 'burden' of the task

Checklists

Ever since Atul Gawande's book, <u>The Checklist Manifesto: How to Get Things Right</u>[13], many lawyers have begun adapting the

---

13 Atul Gawande, The Checklist Manifesto: How to Get Things Right (Metro. Bks. 2009).

logic of checklists to many aspects of their practice, especially for writing documents[14].

Checklists allow you to handle frequently done tasks or transactions more quickly and in the right sequence with more accuracy. If you handle numerous similar or identical matters during the year, you probably have some checklists already, and are reaping their many benefits. But, if you don't use checklists already, start experimenting with them.

Your primary skill as a lawyer is "thinking". Anything that can reduce unnecessary burdens on your thinking will help reduce stress, save time and make you more productive. Checklists help you and your staff to become *consistently* effective. Remember that over time, *most people begin to miss steps*. That is why checklists exist. With checklists, you and your staff members achieve excellence that can be consistently repeated day after day.

A good checklist not only saves time, but it also makes it easier to delegate to someone else when necessary. Here are just a few of the many types of checklists for common legal matters that are regularly used by law firms:
- Consumer Bankruptcy Checklist
- Corporate Checklist
- Criminal Case Checklist
- Defense Checklist
- Personal Injury Action Checklist
- Personal Injury Case Status Checklist
- Purchase of Real Estate Checklist
- Will Execution Checklist

---

14 The Legal Writer"s Checklist Manifesto: Jennifer Murphy Romig, http:// papers.ssrn.com/sol3/papers.cfm?abstract_id=1776107 .

In addition to checklists *for legal matters*, your firm can benefit from creating standard checklists for *conducting operational functions*, like client intake, collecting receivables, engaging outside services, and how to do an after matter review with the client for their feedback on your services.

✁ ✁ ✁

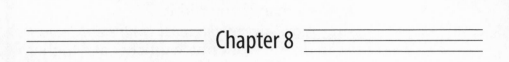

Chapter 8

How to Delegate Effectively

Lawyers commonly mention that they would like to be able to delegate more of their routine tasks, but have a lot of reasons for not doing so. To get a handle on how to delegate more effectively, this section breaks the topic down into its key elements.

Benefits of delegating

Intuitively, you may sense that delegating properly can have a lot of benefits, and you are right! Delegating more can free up immense amounts of your time. Delegating can also keep client fees efficient...you don't want to have a disproportionate number of your hours charged to a matter at your higher hourly rate when some of the work can be done just as well by others at lower billing rates.

Here are more benefits of effective delegating:

1. Frees up your time to spend on business development with your best, most trusting clients. Over 80% of your new business could come from these happy clients, so start there.

2. Keeps client fees efficient by:
   - <u>Passing work down</u> to the *lowest possible level* (where the facts are known, and the judgment is sufficient) where it might take a bit more time, but at an hourly rate enough lower to charge less than if you did it.
   - <u>Passing work up</u> to *the most competent lawyer* who can do the work much quicker at a higher rate, but so efficiently that fees are less than if you did it.

3. Gets results through others, while contributing to their growth in the process. Delegating can build their skills so that they can take on more of the same tasks and more substantive tasks in the future. J. Paul Getty saw it this way:

   "I'd rather have one percent of the efforts of 100 people than 100 percent of my own efforts."

4. Frees your time for alternate better use (Bill it at a higher rate? Work on business development? Apply your time to work that you enjoy more or are better at? Play golf?)

5. Makes finished work yours when you review and approve it.

What to delegate

If you regularly question yourself about tasks that take a lot of your time, it will be easier to decide what to delegate. Ask these questions, and if the answers are "yes", the task in question should be delegated:

1. Does this task require less than my level of knowledge, skill and training?
2. Could I be doing something more important/ valuable than this task?

3. Does this task fit anyone else's position description/ skills/ availability?
4. Is there something of lesser importance/ value can they give up to accept this task/assignment?

Delegate to whom?

The better that the task's requirements match the skills of the one to whom you are delegating, the better results you'll get. That obvious criterion is sometime overlooked in the 'heat of battle'.

So, take a little time to update what you know about the people around you, update what you know about their background and recent work they've done so you will be up to speed on just what skills and experience they actually have. A little time spent on updating your perceptions of those around you can pay off handsomely in improved task/skill matching when you hand off a task.

Another key consideration is to evaluate the likelihood that they will be able to see the task through. For example, if they are already recording their time among several matters for other lawyers and yourself, be sure to get their input on just how they plan to make enough time for your assignment.

Be sure that they check with you before adding any other tasks, especially if doing so jeopardizes your work in any way. Don't assume that they know to let you know BEFORE taking on anything else….request it explicitly. It is easier for them to do what you want if they know exactly what that is.

TIP: If you ask at a matter team meeting *"Who would like to* __(name the task)__ *"*, you might get a volunteer. If the volunteer's skills match the task's requirements, give it to them! A task done by someone *interested in it* will likely be handled much better than by someone NOT interested in it. Plus asking for a volunteer establishes that you don't play 'favorites'.

How to hand off a task

What I usually hear from lawyers is something like this:

> *"I just can't seem to get work I hand off done timely or correctly. I just need a more competent staff...."*

But when I learn exactly HOW the complaining lawyers assign the work, I see that the problem is usually *how the work was actually handed off*. The conversation that occurs when the work is being assigned has a *huge impact* on whether the work gets done right the first time, on time.

So, if you have problems getting the work done right the first time, use these nine guidelines[15] for effectively assigning tasks:

1. <u>Establish a clear understanding</u> of the exact results you expect.
   a. Describe the scope of the *whole project* so they can see where their part or task fits.
   b. Establish a clear picture of the specific <u>results expected</u>, including in what format (i.e., memo, brief draft, Word, table, Excel spread sheet, etc.).
   c. Agree on any special steps or processes to be used.
   d. Give your estimate of the number of hours you think the task should require. If you don't do that, the eager beaver might over-work it and the slacker might under-work it.

2. <u>Leave the method to the doer</u>, to the extent possible.
   a. Have the delegatee explain 'how' they expect to proceed. If they 'create' the method/steps themselves, they will 'own' them, and are more

---

15 Adapted from Ulrich, Paul, *Managing an Effective Legal Assistant Program,* Legal Economics January/February 1979, p. 38

motivated than if they were working just to please your way.

b. Once you know how they would proceed, you can then either agree, or coach them if you prefer different steps/approach.

c. In any case, gain agreement on the steps to be followed, and the chargeable time it should take.

d. A good way to do this on larger tasks is to say *"Why don't you break out the tasks this assignment will require, estimate the hours required for each task, and get back to me. That way we'll be sure we've thought of everything and have a reasonable plan."* When you see their plan, you can approve it, or coach them on any improvements you want. Collaboration like this creates motivation & trust for this immediate and future work.

3. <u>Jointly set deadlines.</u>

   a. A good way is to ask *"I'd like this completed by_____. Will that work for you?*

   b. Then discuss/ negotiate if needed. Usually best when the deadline is set through collaboration instead of by command.

   c. Agree on:

      i. When they are expected to complete the work, and

      ii. When you will review it.

   d. Acknowledge completion, and review when you said you would. Setting the example of meeting your commitments is powerful. It also sets the expectation to be prepared 'on time' for a review.

4. Jointly set progress checks when the assignment is made. Then follow up to *reinforce*, not to *enforce*.

   a. Explain reasons for the progress check (*"to be sure you have what you need…"*)

   b. Setting up those checks/ interim reviews *in advance* lets the delegatee know what to expect. That's better than a 'surprise' drop in on them later to see *"How are you coming on…."* Advance notice avoids your appearing to be the 'cop', or seeming not to trust them or their approach.

   c. It is especially good if you can have the *delegatee initiate* the progress check when it is due, rather than you initiating it. That way, they own the follow-up, and feel more trusted.

5. Permit them to negotiate priorities with you if they feel over-committed to other matters/lawyers to do what you require.

   a. When they lose their right to show the impact of your delegation on their other work, they will feel stressed, and you won't know what they might have to give up in order to do what you are delegating.

   b. This negotiation, when needed, helps you keep their work focused on the Firm's true priorities, not dominated by personalities or ranks of the persons assigning the tasks.

6. Request that they notify you immediately if your deadline becomes jeopardized.

   a. Willing workers most often are reluctant to 'raise the flag' when spotting a possible delay. Instead, they prefer to *"get it back on track"* themselves so as not to look like they *"couldn't handle it"*.

   b. But, if they notify you immediately instead, you can help them work out the best recovery plan, and maybe even command some resources not available to the delegatee for the 'fix'.

7. <u>Remain available to help if needed</u>.
   a. You have as much interest in their successful work as they do.

   b. Their request for help is a coachable moment, pointing out what they can do on their own next time, or assuring them that you care about their success and will pitch in, etc.

   c. Educate them as to where, besides you, they can go for help within and outside the firm. For instance, if your firm has a 'Knowledge Management Portal', be sure all on your teams know how to use it. Be sure all practice group leaders and other subject matter specialists are OK with receiving questions from your team members as needed.

8. <u>Arrange authority</u>
   a. If they need you to arrange more authority for them to succeed, do so. For example, if an associate or junior partner is going to need something from other senior partners, you inform those senior partners that the delegatee is representing you, explain why they are being asked, and encourage them to cooperate.

   b. This *'credentializes'* the delegatee, and removes roadblocks.

9. <u>Teach: final review</u>
   a. For starters, you must review work to ensure quality and value, especially if the delegatee is a paralegal, and you are representing the work as legal work.

b. The final review is also an ideal time for timely coaching or correcting if changes are needed. This is an investment in the professional development of the delegatee.

c. Have the delegatee do the corrections, not yourself. That way they learn, and you save time.

d. Time spent correcting may not be billable, but it is the Firm's legitimate investment in training the delegatee.

How those receiving assignments may see it

It is usually eye-opening to get feedback from those who receive work from senior lawyers or shareholders in a firm. You might be interested in reading Appendix 7. *Typical Complaints of Associates and Staff About How Partners Delegate*. As you look through them, mark any you think might be worth exploring with your own staff. Or, if you're feeling brave, hand them a copy of this appendix, and ask them to identify any that apply to them about *how you delegate!*

You will possibly hear some of the things I have heard, like:

- *"Gives me the assignment, and disappears so that no questions that arise can be answered."*
- *"No deadline is given as to when the work is to be finished. This can result in the assigning lawyer repeatedly checking up with "How are you coming on _____?"*

How to qualify your team members to clients

If the client thinks that you are the only one they can talk to about their matter, it will increase their demands on your time. Conversely, if the client is introduced to those on your matter team, and given the qualifications of each one and what aspect of the matter they are working on, it will be easier for the client to rely on one of the team when you are unavailable.

Other ways to "qualify" your associates and staff are to provide them personalized business stationery and business cards. Well-written bios with a photograph are also superb aids in qualifying professional associates. Besides conveying information about these individuals, those tools somewhat formalize and elevate their status in their own eyes, as well. Great for morale!

Also, put in place specific procedures for managing the possibility that others besides you will interact with the client. For example, make clear exactly what issues each person on the team may discuss with the client. Then, if they talk with the client in your absence, establish in advance just how they are to go about advising you that the contact took place, what questions and answers were discussed, advice given, etc.

The more you can promote the fact that you have a qualified team in place on the client matter, the less time it can take to deal with the client in other ways also. The client will understand that things 'still happen' on their matter even when you are involved in other things. It is also easier to discuss fees when the client knows specifically who are doing work for your approval on their matter(s) and at what hourly rates.

If you want to examine more deeply the interplay between your leadership style and the maturity level of the person being assigned a task, check out the Hersey-Blanchard Situational Leadership Theory at Mind Tools[16].

The theory states that instead of using just one style for delegating, successful leaders should change their style based on the maturity of the people they're leading and

16 http://www.mindtools.com/index.html

the details of the task. A good model there shows how four different styles of leadership interact with four different maturity levels.

❧ ❧ ❧

Chapter 9

How to Improve Client Communication

The goal of this section is to provide you time saving tips on key types of client communication to greatly reduce the time that you'll need to spend in the normal course of matter work. These tips can help you avoid having to deal with client unhappiness, surprises, disputes, failed expectations and unnecessary questions.

You will notice the large role that client expectations have in most of these suggested client communication tactics. The premise is that you are not only expected _to meet client expectations,_ but that you can and should have a major role in _defining client expectations._

As a professional, you are not just an "order taker", implementing only what the client wants and how they want it. Instead, you want to become their "trusted advisor". As such, you retain the right to negotiate client expectations. Done properly, clients respect and appreciate communications that lead to shared understandings of the work that they need you to do for them.

How new client letters can save you time

Usually, you will issue a letter or letters with two types of information for new clients:
- The "New Client *Information* Letter"
- The "Client *Engagement* Letter"

The *"New Client Information Letter"* describes your business practices that govern how you and the client will <u>interact during the conduct of your legal work</u> on their matter. The more that you clarify up front, the better, about your representation, fees, and how to get the best service from you and your firm.

With any new client, how well you work with them to establish expectations will influence greatly just how much time you'll be spending with them to clarify misunderstandings or discuss/debate how matters should have been handled.

When your procedures are discussed before they become an issue, it's easier to establish how to proceed in those areas. This is referred to as "pre-calling", meaning that you discuss your processes for handling potentially sensitive arrangements and reach agreement on how they work <u>before</u> there is a dispute or tension. Then if those issues arise during your work on their matter, it's only an issue of implementing a *previously established* agreement, rather than defensively trying to close some sort of new expectation gap.

For example, one of the most frequent complaints to grievance committees *is failure to return phone calls timely*. The implication of this is that clients have an expectation that is different from the lawyer's practice. The acid test of how good you are at returning calls is that you meet or exceed your client's expectation.

But how often are new clients served without ever establishing what they should expect about when their calls will be returned? And what happens if you are unavailable? This is one area where you can influence their expectation, reach agreement and act on it. Describing in writing 'up front' what your normal practice is for returning calls opens this discussion right away and allows you and the client to agree on it and tailor it, if needed, to each client's particular needs.

Another common oversight is *failing to establish expectations regarding how work outside the original scope will be handled*. Most firms don't have written change order procedures, but I recommend that you establish such a procedure and include it with <u>The New Client Information Letter.</u> That way, you can discuss change orders before it becomes necessary to implement one.

The *New Client Information Letter* should include a clearly worded statement of your preferred procedures in areas like the following:

A. <u>Telephone</u>
1. Taking Calls
2. When I'm Unavailable
3. Emergency Calls
4. Our Professional Staff
5. Best Time to Connect
6. When Calls will be Returned

B. <u>Correspondence And Emails</u>
1. Copies
2. Consulting
3. Emails

C. <u>Fees and Expenses.</u>
  1. Engagement letters
  2. Monthly statements
  3. Advance fee deposits
  4. Reasonableness of our charges / Hourly rates
  5. Assigning work
  6. Change orders
  7. Expenses

D. <u>Results of our work</u>

A template/example of such a New Client Information Letter is in *Appendix 8: The New Client Information Letter Example.* Of course, it is intended to either confirm or start a conversation with your client as to what interactions you have mutually agreed to during the work. So be sure to *discuss it with the client*, and don't just send it to stand alone. The clearer your mutual expectations, the more likely you can meet them and satisfy the client.

The <u>"Client *Engagement* Letter"</u> describes the type of representation you are agreeing to perform for the client. Again, the more specific and thorough the detail of this letter, the easier it will be to administer the work you do to match the work you've agreed to do.

The statement of scope and its budget, if required, are the critical topics in this letter. Sadly, most engagement letters are written too generally, like this example:

> *"Scope of our work. We will handle your file in an appropriate manner and will proceed with legal activities which will, in our opinion, meet your needs and your interests. We may, from time to time, need to seek your instructions and may even ask for them in writing. Please communicate with us often in order to ensure that your needs are met."*

No doubt your engagement letters have evolved beyond that extremely general and passive statement. In fact, some jurisdictions specify what is required in a new client engagement letter about scope of work, such as these example requirements from the D.C. bar[17]:

> *A. Define in detail the scope of the work. Explain what you are going to do and if appropriate, tell what you are not going to do. For example, if you are going to undertake the defense of someone charged with a crime, but you are not going to sue the police over the search and arrest, state that in the agreement;*

> *B. State the fee to be charged. Explain the rate or basis of the fee in detail and give examples where appropriate;*

> *C. Describe the expenses that the client is to pay. In a contingency fee case, detail the client expenses and state whether the client must pay the expenses regardless of the outcome of the case.*

In summary, just remember that the more you can clarify client expectations up front, the more time you'll save. You'll avoid disputes, questions and tension caused by uncertainty of how to proceed or what to expect.

How a scope of work statement saves time

Whether or not your rules of professional conduct require the same level of detail as does the DC Bar, it is probably correct to consider it the minimum standard of care that you should exercise when taking on a new client.

You will note in excerpt "A" above, the importance of assumptions and carve outs: what you are NOT going to do. Key assumptions and carve outs should be enumerated when stating the scope of work because they become

---

17 District of Columbia Bar. *"Example Requirements: D.C. Bar Engagement Letters"*. DCBar Web Site. Accessed 3/3/2013. Web. [See *Appendix 9* for a full copy of this document.]

important in managing any surprises to the scope of work in the future and may be critical to your collecting your legitimate fee.

In order to state the fee to be charged as required in *"B"* above, it is best for the fee estimate to be based on a detailed *work breakout structure* listing individual tasks in time increments as small as you can. This establishes that "reality triangle" showing the closed system of optimum relationships between scope, fee and timing. A detailed task work plan is the basis for stating what will be included and what will be excluded from the work that you are expected to do. (See also **Chapter 7. How to improve Matter Management**)

How to use change orders

Another possible time trap is having to deal with disputes over *changes in the scope of work after the work starts*. It takes less time and tension to deal with "scope creep" if in your engagement letter, you pre-call the method for handling scope changes. So, be sure to state that scope changes will be managed per your *change order procedure*.

That means, of course, that you need a change order procedure. Having a change order procedure written and available for the client to see "upfront" is a requisite to incorporating it by reference in your engagement letter/client agreement. (See more on change orders in the section *How to use Change Orders* in **Chapter 7. How to improve Matter Management**)

When the client signs off on a change order, work can proceed. Expectations will have been clarified and agreed upon, and future time consuming disputes over the fee for this extra work should now be avoided.

How to avoid time traps in estimating fees

For hourly rate matters, of course, you must include your list of hourly rates by rank of those expected to work on their matter: Partner, associate, paralegal, etc. Even for alternative fee arrangements like contingency, fix fee, shared risks, etc., it is vital to have a good internal budget estimate based on expected costs of well-defined and specific tasks needed to do the work. The task-based budget referred to above gives confidence in your price, and is the guide to managing the work throughout the matter, so as to protect your profitability.

Figure 13: The "Reality" Triangle

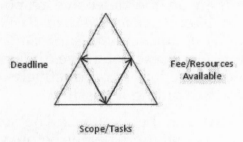

You'll recall the "reality triangle" showing the closed relationship between scope, fee and deadline/timing. Accordingly, the more specific the scope, the more accurate will be your fee estimates/pricing and scheduling. A good scope of work statement also contains assumptions on which the work is based, along with carve outs.

<u>Head off fee confusion.</u> There are three common traps:
- <u>The trap of giving an immediate fee estimate, only to regret it later.</u>
  Sometime a client is insistent on wanting you to *"ballpark"* a fee for a matter they have generally described. You want the work, and you pride yourself on being responsive, so you give what you intend to be just that, a *"ballpark estimate"*. You intend that it will be

subject to revision when you get more facts. You believe that you have communicated this clearly to the requesting party.

The problem is that the client will probably fixate on only the *number* you give, not how you have qualified it. Then, when you get more detail about the work they want you to do, the number you *"ball parked"* could be much less than what will actually be required. The client is (or *claims* to be) *"surprised"*, *"disappointed"* or otherwise *"upset"* at the difference, conveniently forgetting that your number was just a *"ballpark"* number based on some general initial description of the desired work.

You are then on the defensive responding to their comments like: *"...how could that be...but I thought you had a lot of experience in such matters...I don't understand..."* etc. These defensive discussions take time that could be used more productively elsewhere, and so are worth avoiding if possible.

So, how can they be avoided? The somewhat obvious answer is "get more details before you quote a fee estimate." To do that requires courage to resist giving an immediate fee estimate. Instead, negotiate:

> *"I'd love to give you a number immediately, but I would be able to give you a more dependable estimate if I had a little more information on exactly what you want us to do. Then, I'll need some time to think through what would be required to deliver the results you're interested in. Do you have some time now for my questions to clarify?..."*Etc.

Depending on why they want the estimate immediately, you can explain what you need to satisfy their purposes. For example, if they are trying to just put in a placeholder for next year's budget, it is in your interest and theirs that the number is large enough to accommodate the work they had in mind. If it's not large enough, a fee dispute is just getting kicked down the road to when they are ready for you to start the work.

- The trap of quoting a fee range
Since the future cannot be predicted, it's normal to realize that some things may change the initial planned work needed to complete a matter. Thus, the occasional need to quote a fee range is understandable.

But, if you do quote a fee range of, say, $30,000-$35,000 without identifying the assumptions (and carve-outs) on which both numbers are based, you run a credibility risk with your client. If your assumptions are not specified, your client will tend to focus on "... $30,000..."as the probable cost of your assistance. But, you will feel that you can incur as much as $35,000 in fees if needed. So, to eliminate this possible $5,000 built-in fee dispute, specify the assumptions on which it is based:

> *"If we have three depositions or fewer and if we get Judge Adams, I think the $30,000 estimate is spot on. But if more than three depositions are required and we get Judge McGraw, it could run as high as $35,000 or more."*

That way, the final fee will be easier to track to the exact scope of work performed, the assumptions and carve outs, and events that actually occurred.

- The trap of deferring discussion of scope changes.

If the scope of a change is small and the client relationship is a trusting one, it is tempting to think:

> *"I'll just keep good records on this change, and we can discuss it with the client at the end of the matter. I don't want to nickel-dime them with small changes."*

But, a better way to avoid the appearance of *"nickel and diming"* is to agree up front on the threshold amount for aggregated small scope changes, say $2500, which will trigger the need for a change order.

For example, three small changes of $600, $800 and $1200 would exceed a threshold of $2500, and would trigger a client discussion and a change order to be signed or negotiated for all three changes in scope. This approach avoids the perception of nickel diming, but also formalizes how small changes will be handled. Plus, it keeps scope change adjustments current and avoids creating a fee surprise at the end of the matter.

How a communication plan can save time

When a team of more than one lawyer is working on a client matter, the issue of good communication usually needs a bit more formalizing than is common.

Of course, you may have competent talented people working on the client's case and be dealing with competent people in the client's organization. Such was the case in a situation below, but look what happened:

An experienced partner of 33 years in a law firm with over 300 lawyers once told me the following:

"I've been lead partner on one of our big clients for the last 12 years. Recently, the Assistant General Counsel there wanted a quote from us for some new business they were considering giving us. They went directly to one of our partners whom they knew to be in charge of the relevant practice area to get a ballpark fee estimate. The estimate they received was a quick, ballpark number, designated as such at the time.

But the AGC took it to be 'gospel'. The work was awarded 3 months later, but when all was said and done, their bill was four times that 'ballpark' estimate! It took me five or six very tense client meetings and many hours internally to repair this relationship and to establish a new internal procedure for how we go about keeping me involved when giving fee estimates to clients in the future."

As you read that, I'm sure several "solutions" came to mind as to how that could have been handled better. A little planning can go a long way as to how client communications will be handled. It's very helpful to clarify at the beginning of a matter exactly[18]:

- When
- Who
- Is to speak to whom
- About what, and
- How

The experienced partner in the story above was chagrined that the partner who gave the estimate was so willing to "shoot from the hip" without asking more questions and taking more time to do a more detailed task-based work plan. It was little comfort that everyone involved at that time had called this a "ballpark" estimate.

He also was surprised that that quoting partner didn't let him, the client partner, know what was going on with the client request in advance. But he realized that those guidelines had never been discussed or put formally in place.

In other words, there was no *communication plan* established for this matter, with the result that relationships were strained within the firm and between the firm and the client.

---

18 Hassett, Jim. *Legal Project Management Quick Reference Guide, Tools And Templates To Increase Efficiency*, 3rd edition, 2013 Boston, MA. Print. Pages 115-130.

Plus a lot of time was absorbed that could not be billed and could have been avoided with a good communication plan.

Obviously, not every single communication can be categorized in advance. But setting up guidelines, both within your firm and with the client for major communications such as scope changes, fee estimates, material developments, team meetings, etc. will pay dividends in reduced misunderstanding and less time needed to correct them.

So, spend the time to determine what information is needed by the client and everyone on the matter team, how often they need it and the best way to get the information to them. Check with the team and stakeholders regularly for feedback on how communication is going and how communication can be improved. Good communication is the key to optimal matter team performance and to managing client expectations.

What detail is best to communicate with the bill?

The billing-related communication question is whether or not to send them a detailed time listing with each monthly invoice. Of course, they have the right, and should be offered the opportunity, to review all details of their time records any time they wish.

Clients are different, so find out from your client at the beginning of your representation just how much detail they want *with the billing,* while assuring them that the details are available in other ways should they prefer.

Some clients react to seeing detailed time records with the invoice by complaining that 1/10 of an hour entries are "nickel and dime-ing them". Other clients feel that a full detail is necessary with each invoice to establish/verify trust in your billed amount.

The point is, avoid time-consuming discussions or arguments *by letting them choose the level of detail* they want you to provide with their bill. To be safe, don't assume without asking.

❧ ❧ ❧

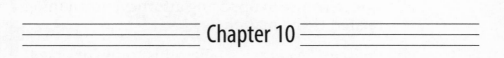

Chapter 10

How to Improve Meetings

Time spent in meetings should pay off in two ways:
- Improve relationships among attendees, and
- Produce effective outcomes, especially on client legal matters

Below are some guidelines you can use as a checklist for your meetings, whether they are virtual or in person, internal only, or with clients.

How a clear meeting purpose benefits all

Client meetings and matter team meetings typically work best when the meeting's exact purpose(s) are clearly <u>stated and communicated</u> in advance to all attendees. Don't just assume that everyone already knows the purpose(s) of the meeting.

When the purpose(s) of the meeting are clear to all attending, it's easier for them to prepare, evaluate the importance of their attendance, etc. Such a purpose statement can include two elements:

- <u>Type of meeting.</u> Generally a client meeting will fall into one of these key categories of meeting type, which can be stated in the statement of purpose for the meeting:

  a. *Decision-Making*: for example, to decide strategy, response to opposing attorney, or anything related to the matter.

  b. *Problem Solving*: usually, this type of meeting is when the answer is not intuitively clear, and clarification of the problem statement and brainstorming its causes and solutions is required. For example, a client thinks your fee is too high, or questions whether arbitration would be the best approach, etc.

  c. *Feedback/Feed Forward:* these types of meetings are primarily for the lawyer to give information to the client or vice versa. In other words, it's for information or education rather than focused on a given decision or problem definition.

  d. *Multipurpose:* this type meeting is, as the term suggests, one where more than one meeting type is involved.

- <u>Specific purpose(s) of the meeting.</u> This is a statement of purpose, starting with *"The purpose(s) of this meeting is (are) to…"* and concluding with a phrase like: *"…review the content of the proposed lease agreement with XYZ Corp. to determine changes needed."*

Sometimes it may seem that writing a statement of the meeting's purpose is simply stating the obvious. But the wording, especially the verbs, govern the boundaries of what is to be included in the meeting and what is to be excluded. For example, if the purpose were simply to *"… Discuss suit-*

ability of XYZ Corp.'s building..." that's a different purpose from *"...approving..."* the lease document's content.

A more general statement of purpose would be less clear, such as this one: *"The purpose of the meeting is to discuss leasing XYZ Corp.'s building."*

A clearly stated meeting purpose gives all parties to the meeting advance notice of what will be covered at the meeting. Then, if they have questions or comments, they can be raised in advance and/or raised at the appropriate time during the meeting.

How to use a meeting agenda

The meeting agenda is <u>the plan for how the meeting's purposes will be achieved</u>.

Ideally, and agenda defines the "straight-line" path from the beginning of the meeting to the end of the meeting regarding what will be discussed. Things not on the agenda will not be discussed unless the agenda is altered ad hoc.

The agenda is also a useful tool to help the meeting leader avoid distractions that might take the discussion off point of the agenda or the meeting's purpose. If you are conducting the meeting, you can defer the distraction by saying something like:

"Well, Adam, (topic of distraction) is not on the agenda, but we could change the agenda to include it now, if you like. Or, possibly it would be better to cover that in another meeting or individually outside of this meeting."

Agendas are easier for attendees to adhere to when they have participated in creating the agenda. It is usually a good idea to run a draft agenda by the client in advance for their review and comment. If that can't be done, then just begin the meeting with a discussion of the agenda, offering an opportunity for attendees to suggest changes. This works well for internal meetings with matter teams as well. Remember when people participate in creating something, they become a co-owner of it and are more likely to protect it, and commit to its success.

Include only the necessary attendees

Meetings are more productive if all necessary attendees are present, and if all the attendees present are necessary. Simply challenge your assumptions as to who is necessary for the meeting to reach its purpose effectively.

A benefit of having only the needed people at the meeting is that the number of communication channels is kept to as few as possible. For example, say that you have three people A, B and C at a meeting. Three attendees require three separate communication channels that must be managed during the meeting, like this:

Figure 14: Three-Party Communication Channels

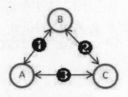

But, if a fourth person, D is added to the meeting, the number of communication channels that must be managed during the meeting, _doubles_ from three to six, like this:

Figure 15: Four-Party Communication Channels

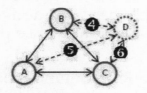

The formula to calculate the number of communication channels possible for any group meeting is N(N-1)/2 where N=the number of people involved.

This same phenomenon occurs internally with the number of personnel assigned to work on a client matter. One must be careful not to "over-lawyer" a matter. What that means is, the larger the matter team, the greater the complexity and the more time spent communicating. Communication is the key to optimal matter performance. Frequently difficulties are often attributed to "miscommunication" or "lack of communication" while working on a matter.

So, optimizing the number of people at a meeting or on a client matter team is important to not only the content of the communication, but also to the complexity of managing that communication among the various channels involved.

Capture outcomes of each meeting

To ensure steady progress from meeting to meeting, be sure to capture the outcomes of each meeting at the end of the meeting.

You may have attended meetings in the past where the first substantial portion of the meeting is spent rehashing what was done at the last meeting, including things that were not followed up on, items that were overlooked or forgotten by attendees, etc.

To avoid that, end each meeting by taking a few minutes to capture (on a flip chart, white board, or projected electronic document) what has been decided or committed to during that meeting and who will be doing what by when and how.

It could also include communication assignments for a "communication plan", and captured like in **Figure 16.**

Figure 16: Template for a Communication Plan

Decided Or Assigned	Responsible Person	Comment/Method	Due Date

Including a write up of these outcomes in your meeting memorandum reminds each attendee what involves them and gives you a track for follow-up and monitoring between meetings, especially matter team meetings. Properly done, the progress status of these outcomes can be briefly reported on at the next meeting, including which are completed, abandoned, on schedule, or needing more time.

⚞ ⚞ ⚞

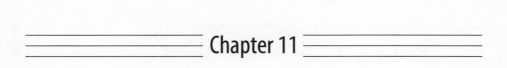

Chapter 11

How to Improve Production of Documents

Producing any document takes time, regardless of the source or sources used and how it is produced. And, with continuing downward pressure on legal fees, you can expect the next challenge to be resistance to paying large sums for merely "papering the deal." The good news is that the main inefficiencies in writing can be overcome fairly easily.

A recent survey[19]asked lawyers to select all sources for writing that that apply to them in answer to this question:

"Which of the following sources are used to draft a legal document?"

The two sources with the highest percentage of lawyers using them are:
- <u>Drafted from scratch</u>: 90% use original legal content specific to the client/matter.
- <u>Used existing</u> documents/ templates: 81% re-use content from a prior matter for the same or different client.

---

19 ALM Legal Intelligence "Meeting Client Expectations? The Hidden Secret for Improved Satisfaction" SPECIAL REPORT January, 2013, p 7

Because those two sources are the most common, anything you can do to improve how you use them when writing will give you the greatest improvement.

How to save time when drafting from scratch

When drafting a document from scratch, the best place to begin is to focus on the outcome you want. An easy way to do that is to take time to *write out a clear statement of purpose* and *the outcome you want* for your document.

For example:

> **"My purpose in writing this document is to_____**
>
> > *...explain how/ why/ etc.*
> >
> > *...persuade them that...*
>
> **"....so that as a result of reading this document, the reader will_____."**
>
> > *...rule in my favor."*
> >
> > *...grant the restraining order."*
> >
> > *...increase their offering price."*

Writing out that clear statement of purpose increases the likelihood that your writing will support it much better than if you just 'know implicitly' what you are seeking.

When you write out your purpose and desired outcome, your *thinking* is refined[20]:

> ". ...*writing does not merely record or communicate, but also* transforms *our thoughts. ...there are two sides to the transformative effect of writing, one connected to communication and the other to external representation:*

---

20 A. Dix (2008). "Externalisation–how writing changes thinking". Interfaces, **76**, pp. 18-19. Autumn 2008. http://www.hcibook.com/alan/papers/. Accessed 26 January, 2013.

- *writing forces processing of your ideas and reflection on them*
- *writing makes your thoughts available as the object of study"*

How to organize your writing process

Next, organize your writing process for greater efficiency and better results. Moving smoothly from one phase of the writing process to another will save much time and increase the quality of your document. Use the 'P.O.W.E.R.' model as a consistent time-saver to efficiently produce improved documents.

Plan:

1. Define your audience and your desired outcome

2. Brainstorm: assemble everything that occurs to you as a candidate to write about

3. Research

4. Define topic statement/main subject, *specifically*

Organize:

1. Do an outline. Here you are sorting and setting categories and priorities. A sentence outline is best, but key-word outlines also work well

2. Assemble your information, sources, evidence, etc.

3. Shut off phone, email, texting, faxes, etc.

4. Close the door/be unavailable

Write:

1. Rough draft/capture ideas-worry about formatting spelling, punctuation, etc. later.

2. Write sections in the following sequence (different from reading sequence)

   a. Body-this is the "what" of your document
   b. Closing – this is your summary and wrap-up of the body's main points
   c. Introduction – you'll write a better introduction after you have defined what you are introducing, i.e. the body and closing.
3. Set initial structure (sequence, headings, bullets, etc.)

Edit/evaluate:

1. Read text as though you were the recipient
2. Adjust sequence and flow
3. Add & delete words, sentences, paragraphs
4. Improve wording and structure

Revise/rewrite:

1. Reword as needed
2. Run grammar and spell check
3. Proof for punctuation, headings, pagination, etc.

A key element in this **P.O.W.E.R.** model is the first step under **O**rganizing: do an outline. If you're not already accustomed to writing from an outline, this may be your biggest benefit, even though it may be the toughest tactic for you to adopt consistently. Initially, you may feel some restlessness and some form of this thought:

"I don't have time to do this outlining… I should be writing the document."

But, think of Lincoln's alleged quote: *"If I had eight hours to chop down a tree, I'd spend six hours sharpening my ax"*.

How to save time by dictating

When your outline is complete in the **P.O.W.E.R.** model above, dictating the original sections of the document is the most efficient way to compose.

Given the large amount of document creation most law practices require, dictating instead of keystroking can be a major time saver. And the technology for doing it gets better every year. If you already dictate, you can skip this chapter, or just review the dos and don'ts it contains to check your own technique.

For example, key stroking/ typing your documents into your computer's word processing program is probably not as fast as you think:

- The average typing speed is 38-40 words per minute (wpm) for adults in a professional working environment (despite many incorrect reports on the web that it is 50-60 wpm).[21]
- In one study of average computer users, the average rate for transcription was 33 wpm, and 19 wpm for composition[22].
- A typing speed above 40 wpm is higher than the average score[23]

---

21 http://wiki.answers.com/Q/What_is_the_average_typing_speed
22 Karat CM, Halverson C, Horn D, Karat J (1999). "Patterns of entry and correction in large vocabulary continuous speech recognition systems". Proceedings of the SIGCHI conference on Human Factors in Computing Systems (CHI '99). New York, NY, USA: ACM. pp. 568-575
23 http://www.learn2type.com/typingtest/typingspeed.cfm

- An average professional typist usually types 50 to 80 wpm[24]

Of course, even at 40 words per minute, keystroking is faster than you can hand-write legibly. The average human being hand-writes at 31 words per minute for memorized text and 22 words per minute while copying[25].

But, you can easily speak at around 250 wpm. In fact, the average adult reads prose text aloud at 250 to 300 words per minute[26].

So, if you dictate at 250 wpm instead of keystroking at 40 or even 60 wpm, you will produce documents _four to six times faster_ . That is _more than significant_, and warrants whatever it takes for you to learn dictation if you don't already dictate.

For our purposes here, it is assumed that you would be using dictation software on your computer or smart phone, allowing direct conversion of voice to text, and NOT that you would record your dictation to be transcribed later by a secretary or transcription service. While that method still beats keystroking your own documents, it is not as efficient or controllable as voice-to-text. And, of course the old school way of dictating live to a secretary is _the most inefficient_ way because it requires two people to be available during dictation.

---

24 Ayres, Robert U; Martinás, Katalin (2005), "120 wpm for very skilled typist", On the Reappraisal of Microeconomics: Economic Growth and Change in a Material World, Cheltenham, UK & Northampton, Massachusetts: Edward Elgar Publishing, p. 41, ISBN 1-84542-272-4, http://books.google.com/books?id=ksxK7J95IF8C&pg=PA41&dq=typists+%22120+words+per+minute%22#v=onepage&q=typists%20%22120%20words%20per%20minute%22&f=false, retrieved 22 November 2010

25 Brown, C. M. (1988). Human-computer interface design guidelines. Norwood, NJ: Ablex Publishing.

26 Ziefle, M. (1998), Effects of display resolution on visual performance, Human Factors, 40(4), 555–568.

How to use "voice-to-text"

Both Word 2007 and Word 2010 have a built-in voice-to-text capability, but they are far from perfect, in that it is virtually impossible to get either to accept both text and formatting instructions directly into your document.

Instead, commercial voice to text software is quite affordable, such as Dragon's NaturallySpeaking versions by Nuance (nuance.com), the provider of Siri to iPhones. They say this about their Legal Edition:

"Designed specifically for the legal community, it automatically formats legal citations, supports third-party correction and provides accurate out-of-the-box recognition of dictated legal terms."

But there are less expensive versions of Naturally Speaking that might serve your purposes.

For dictating on the go, there are a couple of other good products from Nuance: Paper Port Notes for iPad, and Dragon Recorder for the iPhone. Paper Port Notes allows dictating for up to a minute, and editing with the typewriter function. Then, pasting the dictated copy into an email to yourself allows cutting and pasting that directly into a Word document.

However, I prefer the Dragon Recorder for mobile use. It creates an audio recording when dictating to your iPhone. That recording file transfers by Wi-Fi direct to your computer to be transcribed by NaturallySpeaking directly into the document you are using there.

Most of these voice-to-text programs allow you to store common commands and phrases, and continues to update your profile of speaking habits and nuances of your voice. Nonetheless, they aren't perfect... If you say the proper name "Vince" it will probably type out "events". Some such homonyms are a problem, but on balance, the speed and high percentage accuracy is hugely better than old-fashioned keystroking.

<u>Two 'audiences' for your words</u>

Keep in mind that when dictating, you are giving two types of instruction to two different 'audiences':
- The reader: what words the text should say
- The 'transcriber': what formatting you want. This means that you need to have a clear mental picture of the format desired, even at the initial drafting stage. Doing so makes editing later easier.

With a little practice, it will quickly become automatic for you to give spoken punctuation instructions among your text phrases as needed by saying things like: "COMMA", "BULLET THIS", "UNDERLINE THIS", and "NEW LINE".

How to save time using prior work and templates

You probably already avoid "reinventing the wheel" by using templates and prior documents. Documents are individually crafted for unique situations, but there is also a certain amount of commonality and routine content to many documents.

Jim Calloway, Director of the Oklahoma Bar Association Management Assistance Program puts it this way[27] (underlining mine):

"Any error in a legal document could have serious consequences for the client – and the law firm. Still, one can understand frustration with paying a lawyer for proofing

27 Callaway, Jim. "Efficient legal document production for lawyers." lawyersusaonline.com. LawyersUSA, 5 March, 2012. Accessed 26 January,2013. http://lawyersusaonline.com/blog/2012/03/05/document-assembly-for-lawyers/.

and reproofing a document several times. Exceptional law firms will invest the time to bullet-proof the <u>document production system</u>, both to the client's economic benefit and to free the lawyer from the drudgery of re-proofing the same document.

"Clients are always going to be willing to pay top dollar for skilled legal tasks, be that litigation, negotiation, advice or formal opinions from the lawyer. But we will continue to see downward pressure on legal fees and we are going to see more resistance to paying large sums for merely "papering the deal."

In addition to including relevant prior work and templates, there are some technology features that can assist. Here are a few (I have no financial interest in any of them) that are definitely worth exploring:

- <u>Microsoft Word</u> (2007 & 2010): the feature called "Quick Parts" lets you create and store frequently used paragraphs. You can quickly insert them into the document you are writing by clicking the Quick Parts button under "Insert" to see the list of phrases and paragraphs that you have stored there, and select the one you want. Great for personalized client email blasts!

- <u>Pathagoras</u> (Pathagoras.com): They say: *"In just two clicks, using just your existing documents, Pathagoras can present a list of forms or clauses on a designated topic. From that list, you select an appropriate form, clause, or group of clauses to be assembled."*

- <u>HotDocs</u> (hotdocs.com): They say: *"Firms are using HotDocs to generate everything from simple, single-page letters and NDAs to complex contracts and estate planning documents, all in a fraction of the time it would take to do it the old, cut-and-paste way, and with much greater accuracy."*

- The FormTool (formtool.com) They say: *"Whether you design a form from scratch, or use one of over 800 included templates, you can be creating forms in no time at all. With drag-and-drop technology from start-to-finish, FormTool is without a doubt the easiest way to create a professional-looking form."*

The software that you use for timekeeping and to generate client statements probably also includes an "auto complete" function for phrases used in time entry. This allows you to enter abbreviations that will be translated to full-word form on the billing statement. For example, entering the letters "cl ph con" will auto populate in your time record as "client phone conference", saving you 14 key strokes each time. Using hundreds of these shortcuts during a month can save a terrific amount of time. So invest the time to learn them and use them if they are available in your timekeeping system!

How to improve editing effectiveness

To do the best job editing the completed document, I recommend that you print it, possibly with lines double-spaced and edit/proof it from that printed document. Your objectivity is improved by proofing this printed document that you have "never seen in this form before". That way you will catch a lot of things that are more difficult to spot when reviewing your own text on your computer screen. A little objectivity can go a long way to help you reduce your innate tendency to accept your own mistakes by not noticing them. Of course, for quality control, many firms require a final "reading review" by a partner or a trained editor...someone who can stand in the shoes of the intended recipient of the document.

How to improve final reviews by others

The next challenge is to optimize the review process. Ensure that the final document undergoes only the necessary number and intensity of reviews when approving release to the client/ addressee. You don't want to risk any document being delayed or having unnecessary time spent on reviews. But in a recent survey[28], more than two-thirds of law firms cite having between two to five people review a document before it goes to the client.

You may have been party to conversations that include phrases referring to "... the fifth draft versus the six draft...". If so, you were witnessing the dysfunction of a document production system.

The main dysfunction is usually that the first, more senior person to review it does *not* do a focused and thorough review the *first time* it hits their desk. Why is this so? Because, being generally under time pressure to move to their next task at hand, the reviewer is thinking, *"... After all, I'll see it again before it goes out!"*. But, what they overlook in haste now will still be there the next time they look at it.

So, try to get a commitment that the reviewer will take sufficient time to give it "their best shot" in the first instance. (Why does this old saying occur to me now: *"An ounce of prevention beats a pound of cure."*?)

✕ ✕ ✕

---

28 ALM Legal Intelligence "Meeting Client Expectations? The Hidden Secret for Improved Satisfaction" SPECIAL REPORT January, 2013, *p* 8

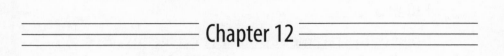

Chapter 12

How to Save Time Dealing With Client Invoices and Receivables

If you have past due receivables, they can take up a lot of time strategizing and implementing collection efforts. Some of the tips for fee estimating and communicating with clients covered earlier can go a long way toward ensuring timely payment of your invoices, avoiding time spent in collecting past due items delayed by uncertainty.

However, here are other tips on how to reduce the chance of late payments and your having to spend the extra time and tension trying to collect them while keeping the client happy:

- <u>Get advance fee payments.</u>
  Having the clients' funds in their trust/escrow account (IOLTA or Regular Trust) saves a lot of time. Be sure to explain that those funds remain theirs in escrow until earned by your firm. These advanced fee payments are a great guard against past-dues. If you aren't already using lawyer trust accounts for holding advanced fee payments, seriously consider using them on your next piece of new business!

- <u>Show the unearned balance in their trust account.</u>

  If you have received an advance fee payment against which you are drawing the earned fees on your invoice, be sure to also show on the invoice the remaining unspent trust/escrow balance net of the current billed amount.

- <u>Specify the payment due date on fee invoices.</u>

  To help avoid that time and tension, put a specific payment due date on your statement/invoice based on the terms of payment that were established in your initial client letter. Such a reminder of the *specific due date* for their payment can go a long way toward getting timely payment.

  What do your invoices now state about *when payment is due*? Is the language specific enough? Here are two examples of phrases that many lawyers use, but which don't help the client know exactly when to write their check:

  - *"Total amount due and payable: $1400.00"*
  - *"Due and payable within 30 days of invoice date."*

  The problem with both of those statements is that they <u>*don't state the date on which payment is expected.*</u> In principle, it is difficult for a client to *meet* your expectation if they don't *know specifically what that expectation* is.

  The first bulleted example above informs the client that it is *"...due and payable..."*, but doesn't ask for it by a certain date.

  The second example above requires the recipient to:

  - Look at the invoice date
  - Add 30 days to it to locate the due date
  - Schedule payment on that date in their calendar

Too much work! The opportunity here is to remove anything that might interfere with quick payment by *stating the payment due date right on the invoice*:

- *"Total amount due and payable by April 6, 2013:$1400.00"*

- *"Due and payable by April 6, 2013."*

Yes, the client *should* recall what payment terms they've agreed to and pay on time. However, human nature being what it is, their individual circumstances are more on their mind at the time they receive your bill than are the terms of your agreement that they signed days or weeks previous!

If you have some clients who are not paying on time, then adding a specific payment date on your bills is one tactic to minimize past-due receivables and the time it takes to collect them.

- State on the invoice whom to call with questions.

Hopefully this will be a name of a person in your office that the client has already met if you have fully introduced your matter team and office support staff to the clients. Showing a name that is new to them can create more questions, and deter them from calling to discuss when they should. Open communications, repeatedly, about fees is one of the keystones to good client satisfaction, and that is encouraged by reminding the client of whom to call with questions addressed to a known person.

- Explain the work you are doing on their matters, and the result you are getting.

When clients understand your work process, they will be able to see how it is benefitting them, and will be less likely to question what you are doing, and the fee required to do it. Using a transmittal letter to explain the results or progress creating the charges for work shown on your invoice may help the client to 'get the picture' of what all that work means in terms of progress on their matter. They are more likely to pay on time if they understand the *value* and not just the *amount* of your fee.

❧ ❧ ❧

Chapter 13

Invest Time In After Matter Reviews

When all work on a client matter is completed and final-billed, it's often difficult to stop and evaluate the total experience. But, investing a little time in an after-matter review can possibly save business and time in the future on similar cases and with this client specifically.

Most importantly, meet with the client to assess their ideas about improving your service. This can be accomplished by a structured meeting with your team and the client to review what worked, what didn't work and what could be done better in the future.

If the client is totally happy with the way things went, that gets reaffirmed, and you and your team can celebrate the praise, which improves morale. Plus, you and your firm get credit for being willing to take the risk of criticism.

But, if there are improvements that need to be made, they can be identified and addressed while they are fresh on the client's mind. Assuring the client of your seriousness to listen and to seek improvements for the future and taking steps to do so can only help solidify the relationship and build trust. Trusting relationships take less time to manage because contentious issues are less frequent.

If you don't find out their dissatisfaction by inquiring, they may never tell you at their own initiative. It is pretty easy for a dissatisfied client to simply move the business to another attorney, leaving you to wonder why *"...we haven't heard from you in quite a while..."*. Remember, the dissatisfied client is under no obligation to tell you. So ASK!!

Timesaving on future matters can be achieved by storing and sharing with others in your firm any tools or arguments that were developed for this case, and which could have application in similar future matters being worked on by others. This can be accomplished by holding a structured meeting with the matter team to identify and capture these items that may help others avoid "reinventing the wheel".

So, invest a little time with your matter team and the client at the conclusion of each matter to conduct an after-matter review to build trust and achieve these longer-term time-saving benefits.

✗ ✗ ✗

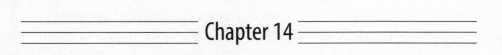

Chapter 14

Time-saving Technology

This book intentionally focuses almost exclusively on personal disciplines, tactics and habits, not technology and tools. Most ideas presented so far can be implemented *on your own* without any major policy changes or additional investment by you or your firm.

Until you develop, and are satisfied with, your own daily personal organization habits, it won't pay to start embellishing them with technology. But a good place to start with technology, is to learn to get the most of the tools already available to you. For example, have you learned how to get the most out of your firm's existing timekeeping system?

Many lawyers I know still have the attitude that they are *"...lawyers, not data entry clerks..."*. They still handwrite time entry details for the day or week on a legal pad, and have their secretary/admin enter them into the *"system"*. Instead, they would be better off learning all their system's key time-saving features themselves, like these examples of how to:

- Use abbreviations that auto-populate completed words into the pre-bill invoice
- Turn phone calls into time records
- Turn calendared meetings into time records

- Use built-in docketing modules to schedule calendar reminders

The only technology-based devices mentioned earlier in this book are your smart phone (To Do List, Daily Plan, email, dictation and Calendar) and your automated time-keeping system (Daily Timekeeping). It is important that you first get fully up to speed on those and your basic computer tools for internet, email, document creation, and scheduling before trying to adopt more sophisticated adjuncts to those basics.

For example, you *could* learn to use iAnnotate PDF[29] for your Android tablet if you don't want to carry a heavier notebook pc when you travel. But, it will not supply you an efficient and effective process for creating and editing documents (this book's P.O.W.E.R. approach in **Chapter 11. How to Improve Production of Documents**) if you don't already have those habits in place with your team. Plus, iAnnotate PDF is harder to use than Word's *Review* tools available on your Surface[30]/notebook/pc and already familiar to you.

But, you are no doubt aware of, and may already be using, other technology that *can* be available *firm-wide* and could have a huge impact on time savings for every attorney in the firm. Case management software is probably the best example, which your firm is likely to have already.

But, if you or your firm's leadership want to dig more into what technology is currently available to improve the firm's time-saving practice management processes, just Google the category phrases below in bold to find the most current sources for that topic's legal tools.
- *__Legal Technology News:__* This online news source provides many links to resources, software, device reviews and editorials. Plus, it contains updates on

---

29 iAnnotate PDF is for reading and annotating PDFs on your Android tablet.
30 Surface is a trademark of Microsoft Corporation.

product releases and white papers on technology topics germane to practice management. www.law.com/jsp/lawtechnologynews/index.jsp

- *__Legal Case Management Software:__* These programs provide efficient ways to create, receive, store and retrieve information on the substance and progress of work on client cases.
- *__Legal Mobil Apps:__* These applications reduce your time and effort to work while out of the office. You'll be able to find what fits your situation for smart phones, tablets/pads, and laptops, and notebooks. (*Dragon Recorder*, for example, for dictating on the run.)
- *__Client Relationship Management (CRM):__* These programs are designed to mine the information you already have on your clients and their industries to help consistently and efficiently establish and maintain trusting relationships and get new business.
- *__Electronic Discovery (eDiscovery)__*: This will take you to sources of software to facilitate electronic discovery, and up-date you on the issues relating to the use of it.
- *__Legal Project Management Software:__* Here you will find a lot about case management, and some emerging software based on the discipline of project management as applied to the practice of law.
- *__Law firm collaboration tools:__* These tools range from firm extranet sites for client access to case records, to web conferencing approaches.
- *__Legal Process Outsourcing__*: This will take you to a lot of information about ways to obtain and manage legal services you may not be staffed to offer in your firm, but need occasionally in order to provide full service to your clients.

- ***Virtual Meeting Technology:*** These sites cover numerous ways you can schedule, conduct, and record on-line meetings for presentations to clients, working sessions among people in scattered locations, etc. Real time and money savers!

✗ ✗ ✗

Appendix 1: HOW TO TAKE AND ANALYZE A TIME LOG

> Where does your time go now? Awareness is the first step in improving your choices.

Overview:

This log is to analyze your ***non-billable*** activities. It is assumed that your ***Billable*** activities are already recorded in your timekeeping system.

It is among these ***non-billable*** activities that you'll find most of what takes your time but does not contribute ideally to the results you want. Therefore, the steps below refer to how to log ***non-billable*** time only.

Instructions:

1. **Choose any three successive working days** while at your regular workplace. Keep the log each day of that period. Use a format like the one on the next page. You may want to keep it as a Word or Excel document , or collected in an approved admin code in your firm's timekeeping system. Keep it visible and within reach, regardless.

2. **For each day, enter your daily plan before your day starts.** Set a deadline time of day for each of your top 4 or 5 key items, billable and non-billable, that you want to accomplish, based upon your best estimate of time required, including contingency for each task/item (i.e., if it will take an hour, leave 1 ¾ or 1 ½ hours available to allow for surprises).

3. **Record each of your non-billable activities** and interruptions *as they occur* during the day. Enter the time

Appendix 1 (Continued)

of day when your *attention shifts to begin working on it*. That is your beginning time. The activity ends when you enter the next activity's beginning time of day.

4. **For each non-billable activity and interruption, state** details such as names, issues, or topics, source, reason. In other words, give as much detail as possible. For example, "Ph C — > John Aaron, re: boat sale" or "Joe B. dropped in re: news on Adams resolution." Use signs and abbreviations (Phone Call out = "C — >" etc.).

5. **At the end of each day, comment on each listed action** with a view toward future improvement where needed. Write suggestions for improvement in the "comment" column, how you could have handled it differently, etc.

6. **When completed,** use the guidelines in **How to Put the Time Log to Work,** on the next page after the time log form.

It is recommended that you repeat the time log one three-day period per calendar quarter. Your benefits:

- You'll discover any barriers that may have crept back into your habits.
- Seeing results from improvements you made will be very satisfying, reinforcing.
- You'll have good data (when needed) to accurately and clearly describe your needs/ timewasters to others, such as to your partners and associates.

Appendix 1 (Continued)

Date: _____

Page 1 of __

DAILY PLAN

To Do	By When?	To Do	By When?
1._____	_____	4._____	_____
2._____	_____	5._____	_____
3._____	_____	6._____	_____

TIME LOG

Time Started	Activity	Comment/Results
_____	_____	_____
_____	_____	_____
_____	_____	_____
_____	_____	_____
_____	_____	_____
_____	_____	_____
_____	_____	_____
_____	_____	_____
_____	_____	_____
_____	_____	_____
_____	_____	_____
_____	_____	_____
_____	_____	_____

Appendix 1 (Continued)

HOW TO PUT THE TIME LOG TO WORK

Time Waster: Anything that keeps you from being able to do your job as effectively as you would like.

To discover your time wasters, answer each question below as specifically as possible as you view your time log. There is no need to write the answers, but do form them specifically and completely in your mind. Make notes on what emerges as one of your top time wasters to work on.

Priorities

1. What time did I begin on the number one priority?
2. How much time (% of total) did I spend on all priorities?
3. Were the unexpected distractions that arose actually more important than what I had planned? Or just more urgent? Or both?
4. How much of the unplanned activities occurring that day could have been prevented by someone else's better planning? Or my own better planning?
5. How much of my day should I have left unplanned and available for unplanned but very important things that are bound to come up: 20 percent? 40 percent?

Interruptions

1. What was the main source of my main interruptions?
2. How long (average) were interruptions?
3. What were main topics or reasons? Were they more important than what I was doing?

Appendix 1 (Continued)

4. Which interruptions could I have avoided?
5. Which important interruptions could I have accepted but shortened by handling them differently?

Delegation

1. What could others have done (within the scope of their duties) and gotten as good or better results?
2. Did this task/involvement require less than my level of training, skill, knowledge and judgment?

Contacts

1. What percentage of my time did I spend with others face-to-face?
2. Which persons am I in contact with the most? Is this OK? If not, can I change it?

Consolidation

1. What activities (calls, visits, letter writing) could I have grouped to be done together?

✄ ✄ ✄

Appendix 2: "TOP 40" MOST COMMON "TIME BARRIERS"

(✓ = Most Common for Lawyers)

Planning

1. __✓__ Lack Objectives/Priorities/Planning

2. _____ Crisis Management, Shifting Priorities

3. __✓__ Attempting Too Much at Once/Unrealistic Time Estimates

4. _____ Waiting for Planes/Appointments/ Courts/ Travel etc.

5. _____ Haste/Impatience

6. __✓__ Interruptions (Telephone Interruptions, Drop-in Visitors, etc.)

Organizing

7. __✓__ Personal Disorganization /Cluttered Desk

8. _____ Confused Responsibility & Authority

9. _____ Duplication of Effort

10. _____ Multiple Bosses

11. _____ Paperwork/Red Tape/Reading

12. _____ Poor Filing System

13. _____ Inadequate Equipment/Facilities

Appendix 2 (Continued)

Staffing

14. __✓__ Untrained/Inadequate Staff

15. _____ Absenteeism/Tardiness/Turnover

16. _____ Personnel with Problems

17. _____ Overly-Dependent Staff

Directing/Doing

18. __✓__ Ineffective Delegation/Involved in Routine Details

19. _____ Lack Motivation/Indifference toward tasks

20. _____ Lack Coordination/Teamwork

Monitoring/ Progress Checking

21. __✓__ Too Trusting of others, don't follow up enough

22. _____ Inability to say "No"

23. _____ Incomplete/Delayed Information

24. _____ Lack Self – Discipline

25. _____ Leaving Tasks Unfinished

26. _____ Lack Standards/Controls/Progress Reports

27. _____ Visual Distractions/Noise

28. _____ Over control

29. _____ Not being informed

30. _____ People Not Available for Discussion

Appendix 2 (Continued)

Decision-making

31. ___✓___ Procrastination/Indecision

32. _____ Wanting All the Facts

33. _____ Snap Decisions

Communicating

34. _____ Meetings

35. _____ Lack/Unclear Communication, Instructions

36. _____ Socializing/Idle Conversation

37. _____ "Memo-itis" /Over — Communication

38. ___✓___ Over-responding to e-mails/ instant messaging

39. ___✓___ Over-responding to voice mails

✗ ✗ ✗

> *"The leading rule for the lawyer, as for the man of every other calling, is diligence. Leave nothing for to-morrow which can be done to-day...."*

Appendix 3: TIMEWASTER ANALYSES

ATTEMPTING TOO MUCH AT ONCE

(Causes: in bold; Solutions: not bold)

1. **Lack of Planning:** Set priorities and deadlines daily. Plan steps to achieve them.
2. **Unrealistic time estimates:** Do matter plans and fee estimates. Analyze under-estimates, then add appropriate cushion. Use change orders.
3. **Starting work late:** Start early. Do a Written Daily Plan the night before
4. **Responding to the urgent:** Be tough in sorting priorities to identify the truly important/vital few vs. the trivial many.
5. **Desire to impress clients and associates:** Negotiate specific due dates and affirm what they *really* want by then, and why.
6. **Being action-oriented:** *Activity Priority Syndrome:* Don't confuse quantity with value, or activity with results. Work smarter, not harder.
7. **Desire to appear cooperative:** Say "No" to lower priorities (Use the 5 steps at *How to Decline Tactfully without Offending*).

INTERRUPTIONS

(Causes: in bold; Solutions: not bold)

1. **Unaware of seriousness:** Take time log of phone calls and drop-in visitors. Evaluate origin, reasons, extent and causes.

Appendix 3 (Continued)

2. **No plan for handling:** Develop plan to screen, delegate, defer & consolidate. Use 'Team Log' and ask others to use it also.

3. **Enjoy socializing:** Minimize, do it elsewhere. Stick to priorities.

4. **Ego. Feeling of importance:** Recognize ego factor. Don't overestimate importance to others of your availability.

5. **Desire to be available:** Distinguish between being *needed* vs. being *wanted* and between being available for business and for socializing.

6. **No plans for unavailability:** Quiet hour; screening; set periods for taking calls.

7. **Desire to keep informed:** Accomplish on planned, more certain basis. Recognize that others may naturally want to keep you informed of everything they are doing, rather than simply the essential results, not activities. Define "in the loop".

8. **Desire to be involved:** Recognize danger of involvement in detail. Divorce yourself from routine matters and details.

9. **Lack of delegation:** Delegate more. Use the nine steps method in *How to Hand Off a Task*.

10. **Over-dependent staff:** Refuse to make their decisions. Encourage initiative. Allow mistakes. Show them where to find info.

11. **Fear of offending:** Don't be oversensitive. Learn to decline when you must without offending. Be courageous enough to do it, suggest your own terms. (Use 5 steps: *How to Decline Tactfully without Offending*).

Appendix 3 (Continued)

INABILITY TO SAY NO

(Causes: in bold; Solutions: not bold)

1. **Desire to win approval and acceptance ("Nice Guy" image):** Recognize possible trap if your desired results are not achieved. You may *lose* respect instead of *gaining* it and become resentful of people who keep asking.
2. **Fear of offending:** Develop techniques of saying "No" without offending.
3. **Belief that agreeableness enhances prospects for promotion:** Learn assertiveness skills-- Read <u>When I Say No I Feel Guilty</u> by Manuel Smith.
4. **Not assessing consequences:** Take a time log recording all "Yes" responses that could have been "No". Assess time wasted.
5. **Lack of reason to say no:** Not wanting to is reason enough. If you say "yes" but aren't interested, you'll probably not do it very well.
6. **Lack of objectives and priorities:** Others will determine priorities for you if you don't have your own. If you don't know what's important it won't get done.
7. **Ambition or desire to be productive:** Better to do less and do it well than to do more and do it poorly.
8. **Autocratic client/partner/tradition:** Balance the trade-offs; what you are gaining in versus what you are losing OR try asking for the right to negotiate.
9. **Thoughtless assumption by others that you will say "Yes":** You likely encouraged this assumption by never saying "No." the 5 steps: *How to Decline Tactfully without Offending.*

Appendix 3 (Continued)

TOO LITTLE PLANNING

(Causes: in bold; Solutions: not bold)

1. **Planning never works out like I plan it, so I quit doing it:** Recognize that the purpose of planning is not to *predict* the future, but to help you manage the future as it unfolds, hour by hour.

2. **Lack system and tools:** Set up personal system: To Do List, Written Daily Plans, Calendar ...and do matter plans.

3. **Lack time to plan:** Make it. Put first things first. Recognize that planning takes time initially, but saves three to four times as much in the execution and gets better results.

4. **Crisis-oriented (assumes crises are unavoidable):** Recognize that amount of time for crises can be estimated. Responding to crises can be planned. Debrief to see how to avoid after each one. Plan better.

5. **Lack self-discipline:** Set deadlines for yourself for priorities; do daily plan for one month.

6. **Fear of commitment**: Recognize that while objectives mean commitment, they also mean knowing when you have succeeded. No commitment=no focus=no power to achieve.

7. **Difficulty assigning priorities to tasks:** Not easy, but very productive. Try one of the methods described in this book.

Appendix 3 (Continued)

SOLUTIONS for DROP-IN VISITORS

1. Authorize your secretary to set up future appointments.
2. Close your door when you need to concentrate, and explain what it means.
3. Meet outside your office.
4. Announce your 'quiet times' ahead.
5. Confer standing up.
6. Have visitors screened.
7. State a "Time limit" on the visit.
8. Go to their office.
9. Have secretary monitor visits, interrupting after agreed-upon time.
10. Use a 'hideaway'.

✗ ✗ ✗

Appendix 4: PLANNING MODEL FOR A LAW PRACTICE

Figure 17: Brave Words vs. Crude Deeds

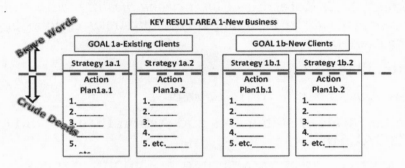

EXAMPLE

KEY RESULT AREA (KRA) 1: *Increase the Firm's number of matters from banks.*

GOAL 1a: *Obtain five new matters from existing bank clients in our region this quarter.*

Strategy 1a.1: Existing Clients-*Conduct three "off the clock" meetings per month for this calendar quarter with existing bank clients to discuss their needs with the aim of uncovering referrals and new business with existing bank clients. These include after matter reviews of matters closing during this period.*

Action Plan 1a.1

1. *Matter XYZ Corp. wraps up March 2nd, so plan an after-matter meeting.*
2. *Ask Randall, Adams, and Koch to attend from our firm.*
3. *Ask GC who should attend from XYZ Corp. Need only 3 people.*

Appendix 4 (Continued)

4. *Set date.*
5. *Arrange to hold in their bank conference room if possible. If not, get consensus on site.*
6. *(–n more steps are required for setting the agenda, arranging refreshments, audio-visual support, handouts, follow up methods, etc.)*

Strategy 1a.2: Referrals- *Conduct one meeting per month for this calendar quarter with non-client banks referred to us by our happy clients.*

Action Plan 1a.2

1. *(–n steps similar to AP 1a.1 above)*

(Similar **Strategy** statements and **Action Plans** would exist for **GOAL 1b**)

PLANNING OBSERVATIONS and DEFINITIONS

1. This classic planning structure (KRA→Goal→ Strategy→Action Plan) shows what is needed to attain any major results you want for your firm or practice area.
2. KRAs are *general statements of the categories of results* desired: *"…number of matters for banks…"*
3. Goals are the *specific statements of the desired results*:*"…five new…existing clients…our region…this quarter.* "It is a good idea to apply the following criteria to any goal statement: is it **S.M.A.R.T.**?

> **S**pecific
>
> **M**easurable
>
> **A**chievable
>
> **R**esults-oriented
>
> **T**ime specific

Appendix 4 (Continued)

4. The "Brave Words" label applies to all information above the red line, since those are simply aspirational statements. The biggest single barrier to attaining a goal is that no action plan is created showing the steps taken to reach it. Until the "Crude Deed" action steps are taken as listed in the "Action Plans", progress doesn't happen. Each step in the Action Plan is scheduled in the lawyer's Written Daily Plans and executed. If it is not in the daily plan, or a calendared self-appointment to work on it, it probably won't happen.

5. One frequent criteria when assigning task priorities is to ask whether or not it is <u>linked to a Firm or Practice Area Goal</u> just as the above example Action Plan tasks are linked to the Goal to *"Obtain five new matters from existing clients this quarter."*

6. Notice that, in this example, two Goals for one KRA end up with four Strategies, each with Action Plans that could contain 10+ tasks each. That could add up to a total of 40 tasks for that one KRA.

POINT: BE CAREFUL! *Pursue only a few goals at any one time.* You must be realistic about how much time you can invest in each. Pursuing goals usually takes more time than you initially expect once you list the steps needed to achieve them (i.e., create the Action Plans for each Strategy). So *keep Goals few and meaningful* to be realistic.

꒰ ꒱ ꒰

Appendix 5: PROFESSIONAL SCREENING

(Planned, Selective Availability)

Rationale

Personally answering every phone call or accepting every unscheduled drop-in visitor gives the caller (anyone with your ten digits or knowledge of your location) the right to set your priorities. Sticking to priorities demonstrates that you try to give quality time (uninterrupted) to each matter you work on. So, deferring callers that do not need immediate attention or are lower priority helps you stick to your true priorities.

The Fear of Offending

Naturally, being available for every caller would be ideal if every call needed immediate attention. So the trick is to be able to avoid selected calls and avoid offending by meeting these three criteria:
- Decide to be available or not based on the issue, not on the person calling
- Defer lower priority topics/calls
- Satisfy every caller by ensuring that their business gets handled timely, even if not immediately
- Allow true emergencies and VIPs to override

The Method

Here is a proven script for professional screening that meets the above criteria. It requires that a 'live' person answer and use the script. Also required are pre-established supporting arrangements that must be made by the lawyer and the screener to make it work.

Appendix 5 (Continued)

Of course, there are other possible caller responses than the ones shown, but the main ones are there for you and your screener to learn and build on.

The Result to expect

A large percentage of callers will learn to rely on the professionalism of your office when they are greeted tactfully, are dealt with using an attitude of helpfulness, and receive call backs when promised.

Habits that help professional screening to work best are:
- Setting and sticking to daily priorities
- Legitimizing the right to defer and call back or refer to someone else to handle
- Being tactful so as not to offend
- Returning all calls when promised

About This Script

The scripts below shows what the screener says in the numbered steps. Under that screener script appears a description of the support arrangements that *must* be made in advance, labeled as:

a. *Lawyer must:*

b. *Screener must:*

Those "must" steps are required for the screening to work tactfully.

Immediately after those *"musts"* appears what the <u>caller</u> says, followed by the <u>screener's</u> response as the next step, and so on throughout the script.

Appendix 5 (Continued)

SCRIPT FOR PROFESSIONAL CALL SCREENING

I. <u>When caller is largely cooperative</u> **(See II. Below for when the caller is NOT cooperative.)**

1. *Hello: Boyd, Dewey, Winnem & Howe, this is _____(name of screener)...*

   a. *Lawyer must:* Authorize the screener to use their first name with each caller.

   b. *Screener must:* Remember to state their own first name. Callers are more cooperative if they hear a voice with a name attached.

"I need to speak to Lawyer_____" – Or-- "Is Lawyer_____ in?"

2. *She is in and ("and" not "but") she is unavailable until XX:00 o'clock. May I help you?*

   a. *Lawyer must*: Tell the screener when she'll be available/ will be returning calls. That specific information creates caller trust in your purposefulness. Also needs to authorize the screener to offer help. Qualify your support/ screener to all clients so that clients will trust anyone on your staff to tell them anything about their case. May require telling clients that staff adhere to the same code of professional confidentiality that you do. May have to train clients to tell screener details.

   b. *Screener must:* Provide a direct answer to caller's direct question: *"Yes..." or "No...".* No lying is needed, because it is okay for the lawyer to be "in" and also be "unavailable". Also be willing to help. Sometimes it is in your job description to help protect Lawyer's time. Sometimes, others may be asked to protect your time.

Appendix 5 (Continued)

"No, I really need to speak to her!"

3. *Ok...I can arrange that... May I say who is calling?*
    a. *Lawyer Must:* Provide screeners with list of VIPs-people you will interrupt for whenever they call.
    b. *Screener Must:* Be comfortable asking. It is a legitimate business requirement to know who is calling and for what purpose....**so you can put through the ones that should be put through.** You may have to explain why you are asking: *"I'm asking so that Ms. Boyd can be ready with the file when you and she do talk."* This may be a VIP, whom you would put right through.

"This is Marv Ashraf."

> *If Marv <u>is</u> a VIP, go to step #8*

> *If Marv <u>is not </u>a VIP, go to step #4*

4. *May I ask the nature of your call? (The topic you would like to discuss?)*
    a. *Lawyer must:* Let the screener know what you are working on (no. 1 Priority) so that they can compare what this call is about with what you are doing, and make a decision for you as to whether to interrupt or take a call-back.
    b. *Screener must:* Be comfortable asking, and use the exact words in the script (reduces chance offending). The reason you need to know the topic is to help you get the caller and Lawyer together to talk in a timely way.

"It is about my hearing date...I've developed a conflict". (See section II below for how to respond to a caller who is less cooperative in giving their reason for calling.)

Appendix 5 (Continued)

5. *I will let her know that you have discovered a conflict. She will be returning calls between ___ and ___ or between ___ and ___. Would you be available for her callback at one of those times?*
   a. *Lawyer must:* Inform the screener the times you have set aside (and actually use) for call-back times daily. If messages do not get returned, the system loses credibility, and all callers will learn to try to break through the screener rather than wait for your call back.
   b. *Screener must:* Know when (even ask and prompt Lawyer to give you those times) Lawyer will be making call backs. Knowing the time specifically for call backs can eliminate telephone "tag".

If response A: *"Neither of those will work for me...."*, go to step #6.

If response B: *"Ok, between ___ and ___ would be best for me."*, go to step #7.

6. *When would be the best time for you, and I will put that on the message?*
   a. Lawyer must: Read the suggested time on the message, and either get back then, or **have someone call then to reschedule a phone appointment.**
   b. Screener must: Remember to ask the caller for a specific time to put on the message. That reduces telephone tag

7. *Thanks for calling. I will take this message right in.*
   a. *Lawyer must:* Review messages frequently to see what is pending (names and topics to help set/revise daily priorities). Make calls at promised times, have someone call back where not promised, but requested by client.

Appendix 5 (Continued)

    b. *Screener must:* Remind Lawyer of the promised call-back times in advance of them

Step 8 below is used after step 3 if that step determines that the caller is a VIP.

    8. *Oh, Mr. Ashraf…She did want to be interrupted for your call. One moment, and I will put you through!*

        a. *Lawyer must:* Stop what you are doing and take the call since it is from a VIP. Otherwise, the screener has misled the caller.

        b. *Screener must:* Know the VIP list for the day, and put them through enthusiastically. That makes them feel special, since you've already said the lawyer is unavailable.

II. <u>When caller is non-cooperative on giving name and topic</u>

(Use the firsts 3 steps under section **I.** *…***where caller is largely cooperative**)

    4. *May I ask the nature of your call? (The topic you would like to discuss?)*

        a. *Lawyer must:* Let the screeners know what you are working on (no. 1 Priority) so that they can compare what this call is about with what you are doing, and make a decision for you as to whether to interrupt or take a call-back.

        b. Screener must: *Be comfortable asking, and use the exact words in the script* (reduces chance offending). The reason you need to know the topic is to help you get the caller and Lawyer together to talk in a timely way.

"She knows what it is about…!!!"

Appendix 5 (Continued)

5. *I'm sure she does...but she will ask me. Can I please tell her so she can be ready with an answer when she calls back?*

    a. *Lawyer must:* Permit and encourage the screener to go this extra step to educate the caller. This is one caller that you may later have to coach on how to leave a message, that your support people are trustworthy, that screening is to help get them through to you quickly as soon as really needed, etc.

    b. *Screener must:* Be brave enough to say these words. Hardly any caller would say in response: *"No, I'd rather you swing in the wind on that one!!!"*

✂ ✂ ✂

Appendix 6: KEY BENEFITS of MATTER PLANNING

1. Discourages procrastination by identifying the first steps as isolated steps, easy and do-able, as opposed to considering the "whole thing at once".

2. Gives a better estimate of time required (usually identifies that more time than expected will be needed). Allows more accurate fee estimating/ client expectations.

3. Helps anticipate cost or fee problems and delivery problems.

4. Provides useful feedback to others of true complexity required. (Example: Client gives unrealistic deadline, but the matter plan will show what is actually required.)

5. Causes you to "think it through".

6. Allows you to establish a logical sequence for the steps.

7. Pinpoints missing steps.

8. Identifies the people, material and other resources to be needed and when.

9. Identifies the commitment needed from others and yourself.

10. Identifies the potential obstacles or problems that may need to be solved. (Risk planning)

11. Demonstrates the real degree of attainability--in other words, makes the case or matter more realistic.

12. Establishes a clear beginning and ending point.

13. Identifies tasks and general areas of responsibility that can be delegated.

Appendix 6 (Continued)

14. Helps identify additional goals or related achievements.

15. Shows where expert input/ client help will add value.

16. Identifies the elapsed time required, i.e., total number of days from the beginning of the matter or phase to its end as influenced by the need to wait or process certain interim steps.

17. Allows insights as to which steps can be consolidated to gain efficiency.

18. Becomes a checklist to monitor progress of yourself and others.

19. Allows you to test consistency of this matter with your other goals.

20. Stimulates seeking simpler ways.

21. Clarifies potential end result which has an impact on steps taken to reach it.

22. Identifies areas where unknowns exist and contingency plans can be developed.

23. Identifies steps that can be in progress concurrently.

24. Makes the case or matter seem more "familiar" and therefore arresting of attention.

25. Identifies real staff "matches" or assignments needing to be changed in order to gain efficiency.

26. Reduces anxiety over undone details. Those are now written and are available for reference.

27. Increases client understanding as to what is required to meet their desired results.

✄ ✄ ✄

Appendix 7: TYPICAL COMPLAINTS[31] FROM ASSOCIATES AND STAFF ABOUT POOR DELEGATION OF TASKS by PARTNERS

1. No deadline is given as to when the work is to be finished. This can result in the assigning lawyer repeatedly checking up with "How are you coming on _____?"
2. Requested work is to be done "as soon as possible", generally understood to mean "Stop whatever you are doing and do this". It implies further that the partner has no interest in what competing commitments may be on my schedule.
3. Deadline given is a 'false' deadline, meaning that I strain to meet the given deadline, only to find out that my work is not even looked at by the assigning lawyer until much later than requested. The resulting feeling is that I have been manipulated to deliver within unnecessarily short lead time for no reason. This undercuts trust in the validity of the next such deadline given by that lawyer.
4. Incomplete information needed to do the job assigned, only to discover later that the info was in the lawyer's possession all along.
5. When tasks are assigned, the lawyer doesn't tell me what the background is, what is to be done with the finished work, etc.

---

31 These comments have been accumulated over the years by my unpublished surveys of associates and staff conducted in connection with consulting engagements with individual law firms on practice management topics.

Appendix 7 (Continued)

6. I don't know exactly how my work 'fits in' with other, successful legal work for the client or how it will be used, etc. This can lead to my feeling like a pieceworker, not trusted to know the fuller context and value of my work.

7. Short lead time is given from assignment to due date, but only because the lawyer 'sat on it' several days after it could have been handed off to me. This creates a feeling of "I could do better work if the lawyer would get organized" and "It isn't fair for their oversight to cause me unnecessary pressure."

8. Unrealistic expectation as to how much chargeable time the assignment should take. Assigning lawyer says "should take you only a couple of hours." but it really takes 10 hours under the best of circumstances. Leads to my feeling that "nothing is impossible for the person that doesn't have to do it." Makes me appear incompetent.

9. Puts me into the unsupported position of being inept. Would rather be able to review the assignment, and then go back to compare the lawyer's basis for the short estimate to my work plan so a shared expectation could be created.

10. Assignments come to me without going to our department head, who needs to know so that our work load can be balanced, and our priorities are known and protected. This puts me in a position of surprising the department head with workload not anticipated by the department head when other commitments are being made by them at the same time.

11. Gives me the assignment, and disappears so that no questions that arise can be answered. This delays work on the matter, creates tension between lawyer and me when I have to "track down" the lawyer and press for needed information.

Appendix 7 (Continued)

12. Changes instructions in midstream without any change in circumstance, except that the lawyer "changed my mind." Could have been avoided with more forethought before giving me the assignment. I feel that more discussion at the time of hand-off would solve this.

13. On the same component of the same matter, different lawyers give contradicting instructions. This leaves me feeling that "they don't communicate" between themselves. Discouraging.

14. No feedback on my work after it is turned in. Would like to hear "Nice job!" or "Couldn't use it, and here's why..." or something rather than nothing. Leaves me with the feeling that my work is unimportant. Appreciation or correction is preferred to silence. I want to please, but can't tell if I do or not.

15. A few weeks after work is turned in, the same assignment is received again as though I never provided the work in the first place. It is unclear if the work was lost, or what. Leaves me with the perception that the lawyer is disorganized.

16. Assigning lawyer will just grab whoever is available at the moment, regardless of the appropriateness of the level of work to the level of my experience.

✗ ✗ ✗

Appendix 8: NEW CLIENT INFORMATION Letter

<u>Use as companion to/part of the Engagement Letter</u>

(Contents to be personalized for each client.)

(Adapted from letter developed for ARN, MULLINS, UNRUH, KUHN & WILSON, Wichita, Kansas)

I. TELEPHONE CALLS

When you call, I will try to take your call immediately. Our fee for phone calls is based on the time spent on the phone call, rounded to the nearest one-quarter hour. Our minimum increment for a phone call is one-quarter hour.

If I am not available to take your call, I will try to return it promptly, generally within two hours. When I am unavailable, remember that it is only because I am keeping a commitment to you or another client. When working on a matter for you or another client, I tend to complete tasks that require undivided attention before taking or returning calls. These deferred calls will be returned within 24 hours of their receipt.

True emergency calls will always interrupt meetings with other clients, drafting documents or briefs, or other work that otherwise would require undivided attention. You and I will work out a definition of "emergencies" to your satisfaction.

Our paralegals, secretaries and receptionists understand and subscribe to the same code of professional confidentiality that lawyers follow; therefore, please give them (or leave

Appendix 8 (Continued)

on my voice mail) all the particulars of your call: subject, issues, timing factors, your phone number, the best time to reach you that day-anything you think would expedite our getting back to you prepared to talk. That way, they can help get your matter to my attention, or to another member of your matter team, at the earliest moment required. If they do not know the substance or topic of your call, it makes it more difficult for us to give it the priority it requires. Please give your phone number (although we have it in our files); that also expedites our calling you back.

The best times to connect with me are during normal office hours, 8:30 a.m. to 5:30 p.m. I usually take lunch from 11:30-12:30. There are times during the week when I usually have calls deferred:

- ✓ Monday mornings: typically spent organizing work for the week and putting out 'brush fires' that have arisen over the weekend.

- ✓ Friday afternoons: usually spent concluding projects worked on during the week to be sent out in the evening mail.

II. CORRESPONDENCE and E-MAILS

You will receive copies of virtually every document I receive or produce concerning your case, particularly correspondence that involves other parties. Similarly, I will need to see certain correspondence that you might receive, as we mutually agree.

You will be consulted with respect to every major decision affecting your case. We will make every effort to keep you well informed of the progress of your case. Please let me know if you should ever feel over-informed or under-informed; after all it is your case.

Appendix 8 (Continued)

If your matter is litigation, you will be notified of any large volumes of documents received from opposing counsel (such as in response to a request for documents). Rather than making copies of these for you at your expense, we will make arrangements for you to review them in our office if you prefer.

E-mails are certainly encouraged, but I consider them to be best for transmitting material of a "for your information" nature as attached documents (PDF, Word, etc.), and for information that does <u>not require discussion or an immediate response</u>.

My assistant reads all my email, and helps me prioritize them periodically during the day. Therefore, it helps if each email has its own, specific subject line with the topic and timing for handling included. All emails will be responded to within 48 hours. If it is more urgent than that , or requires discussion, I suggest using the telephone.

III. FEES and EXPENSES

The cost of engaging our services comprises several elements, such as: the scope of the engagement (our work), the letter confirming that work, monthly statements, retainers, reasonableness of our fees, and expenses. Each of these is discussed separately below.

Engagement Letters

To engage our services on any matter we need you to review and sign an Engagement Letter (enclosed). It outlines for you the scope and extent of our employment and our fee arrangement. This Engagement Letter is primarily to help ensure good communication from the start. It also conforms to both the ethical requirements of our profession and requirements of our malpractice insurer.

Appendix 8 (Continued)

Monthly Statements

Unless otherwise provided in the Engagement Letter, you will receive monthly statements itemizing charges for services rendered and expenses that we have advanced, along with our comments on how we are progressing, what the work described means to your matter, etc.

Amounts are payable upon receipt. We appreciate prompt payment, as we have payroll to meet and bills to pay just like any other business.

Advance Fee Deposits

In the majority of cases that we handle, an advance fee deposit is required before we incur any professional fee or expenses on your behalf. Fee deposits are to ensure payment for our services, and your commitment to the matter. They also reduce the likelihood of embarrassment that can occur over collection of past due amounts. Such advance fees are not our property until earned, but will be put into an escrow account for only your use. Of course, any unearned advance fee amounts at the conclusion of your work will be returned immediately.

Reasonableness of Our Charges

You will always find lawyers who charge more or less than we do for a particular service we offer. However, our charges are competitive with rates charged by other attorneys in this geographical area who have our level of experience. You are always entitled (and we will make every effort to provide you) a full explanation of your bill, so please do not hesitate to contact us should you have any questions.

It is my practice to assign all client work to the professional whose fee level and experience will get the desired results. This is one way of ensuring you quality professional attention at the lowest available cost, under my close supervision.

Appendix 8 (Continued)

Emergencies and/or last minute requirements outside the scope of our agreed upon work will incur additional, and possibly higher than normal, fees to accommodate the situation. The need for such exceptional service will be agreed upon in advance, case by case, as it arises, according to our written change order procedure.

Expenses

We will, in all likelihood, incur expenses on your behalf for which we will expect you to reimburse us. Examples of these expenses are as follows:

- ✓ filing fees and court costs

- ✓ court reporter charges

- ✓ costs of transcripts, postage and copies

- ✓ mileage, meals and lodging if the matter requires travel out of town

- ✓ fees for expert witnesses and consultants

If your case at the outset appears that it will involve these expenses, we will require an advance payment at the time we take your case. We will invoice you immediately for expenses that we advance if :

1. You have not given us advanced payments, or
2. If the advance payment has been depleted

We may request that you pay the provider directly if we feel we are not in a position to advance such expenses on your behalf. If you have a question concerning what expenses your case will involve please ask us.

Appendix 8 (Continued)

IV. RESULTS

The canons of our profession and the uncertainties of life prohibit us from guaranteeing any specific results. The law is extremely (and increasingly) complex; and it is not an exact science. Additionally, a small change in facts can greatly alter the outcome of your case from a similar case being used as a precedent. We will use our very best efforts to pursue your objectives within the bounds of the law and the lawyer's code of ethics.

We appreciate your suggestions. We are continually looking for ways to serve our clients better in a prompt, courteous, and cost-effective manner. When we succeed in serving you satisfactorily, we would appreciate your referring us to others; a lawyer's best source of new clients is referrals from existing clients, and we try never to forget that. Should you ever feel that your expectations are not being met, please let me know, so we can work it out if at all possible.

Thank you for your trust in us for your legal matter. I look forward to working with you and putting our firm at your disposal.

Attached, is a roster of our key personnel, with names, functions, and phone numbers for your convenience. Also attached is your engagement letter. Please read it carefully

Appendix 8 (Continued)

and sign and return it in the enclosed envelope by (_date) along with a signed copy of this letter.

Yours Truly,

Robert Boyd, Partner
Boyd, Dewey, Winnam & Howe

✄   ✄   ✄

Appendix 9: Example Requirements: D.C. Bar Engagement Letters

[Source:http://www.dcbar.org/for_lawyers/bar_services/ practice_management_advisory_service/engagement_ agreements.cfm]

The Elements of Engagement Agreements and Letters

The essential elements to a bullet proof engagement agreement between a lawyer and a client are the following:

First, have a conversation with the potential client about fees, how you work, your ground rules, the client's expectations, what you expect of each other, and how you will communicate. Do not rush this exchange. Allow for the free flow of information. Arrive at an understanding and say it out loud.

Second, assuming you have an understanding and intend to proceed into a lawyer/client relationship, prepare a written engagement letter that does the following:

A. Define in detail the scope of the work. Explain what you are going to do and if appropriate, tell what you are not going to do. For example, if you are going to undertake the defense of someone charged with a crime, but you are not going to sue the police over the search and arrest, state that in the agreement;

B. State the fee to be charged. Explain the rate or basis of the fee in detail and give examples where appropriate;

C. Describe the expenses that the client is to pay. In a contingency fee case, detail the client expenses and state

Appendix 9 (Continued)

whether the client must pay the expenses regardless of the outcome of the case.

When you have not regularly represented the client, the above three elements are required in a written engagement letter by the **District of Columbia Rules of Professional Conduct**.[1] If the case involves a contingency fee, a written agreement is required.[2]

It is of course the best practice to use a written fee agreement in every case that the lawyer and client sign and to address in clear, simple language other issues such as the following:

D. Fee arbitration: In D.C., a lawyer may have a provision in a fee agreement that any fee dispute be submitted to the **D.C. Bar Attorney/Client Arbitration Board** provided the written agreement informs the client that counseling and a copy of the ACAB's rules are available from the ACAB staff and provided the client consents in writing to the mandatory arbitration.[3] When the client requests arbitration of a fee dispute, the lawyer must arbitrate.[4] If the lawyer requests arbitration, the client may elect to participate.

E. Detail what is expected of the client: Explain what cooperation is needed and expected. Explain how you will communicate and what the client can expect regarding phone calls, email, letters and meetings.

F. Address your right to withdraw and the client's right to terminate the relationship.

G. Describe your intention to use an associate, paralegal, or contract lawyer and how you will charge for this assistance.

H. Make clear that you are not guaranteeing a result, and receive an acknowledgement from the client that no result is promised.

Appendix 9 (Continued)

I. Address how, when the representation ends, you will deal with the client's property and the file. The file belongs to the client with one exception.[5] If the client does not request the file, the lawyer must retain it for at least five years.[6] Consider copying or scanning the file if the client requests the file, and if the lawyer retains the file for five years, allow in the agreement for the right to destroy the file. Depending on the case and nature of your practice, it may be wise to keep a file longer than five years, or to routinely scan the file and return original documents to the client.

J. Put a limit on the time period for the client to sign and return the agreement. Especially when time is of the essence, insist that in order for an attorney/client relationship to proceed, a signed copy of the agreement must be returned by a specific date. Calendar that date and if the individual continues to be nonresponsive, confirm in writing that no agreement has been reached.

As with any well drafted agreement, clear, simple language that details the terms and gives examples will go a long way to avoiding disputes. For example, consider the following:

K. If the representation involves litigation, does the scope of the work cover an appeal? If you are excluding an appeal from the scope of the representation, make it clear that negotiating a new agreement will be necessary for an appeal.

L. How will the selection and payment of an expert witness or investigator be addressed?

M. If it is a flat fee case, state precisely what will be done for the flat fee and whether the start of work is contingent on the fee being paid. If it is an advance fee, explain how you will be charging against the advance fee and what happens or is expected of the client when the advance fee is exhausted. Explain that any unearned fee will be returned.

Appendix 9 (Continued)

Fee advances and costs are the property of the client until they are earned or incurred unless the client gives informed consent to a different arrangement.[7]

N. If it is a contingent fee, explain how the fee will be calculated in the event of a settlement or collected verdict. Is the fee calculated against the gross settlement or verdict, or are expenses paid or reimbursed before the fee is determined?

O. It is best to explain that unearned fees and unincurred costs will be placed in your trust account and withdrawn as earned and incurred.

P. If you are billing on an hourly basis, it is best to explain how your time on all aspects of the case will be billed by giving examples, such as preparation for a hearing, research and investigation, drafting a motion, taking a deposition, and examining records. Explaining in detail in the bill itself what you are doing and the result you are obtaining can help the client understand the process and be less likely to question the bill. If you intend to charge a minimum billing increment for phone calls and letters, it must be stated in the agreement.[8]

Q. Detail how you will cover both inside and outside costs. Inside cost examples are postage, copying, and long distance charges. Outside cost examples are filing fees, messenger expenses, process fees, and court reporter charges. If you intend to pay all costs and pass them onto your client in the bill, explain this in detail. If you elect to have the client pay all outside costs directly, this must be set out in the agreement.

R. If the lawyer pays the costs and disbursements related to prosecuting a case with a line of credit, the lawyer may pass the cost of the line of credit on to the client provided the client has been informed in advance and agrees, and provided the expense is reasonable and the lawyer has maintained a

Appendix 9 (Continued)

separate accounting. The costs must be directly attributable to the client and not simply overhead expense.[9]

S. It is advisable to explain your billing practices and state when the client can expect to receive the bill, who to call with questions, and when payment is due.

T. The agreement should have space for both the lawyer and client to sign and date the agreement and each should have a signed original.

Disengagement or termination with the client should be memorialized in most circumstances by a letter stating that the legal representation has ended. When the matter is complete, send a letter that:

A. Thank the client for the opportunity to have been of service and state that the case is over and no further work will be performed. Explain why;

B. Addresses the return of client property and how the file will be handled. See paragraph I above;

C. Acknowledges any other terms or conditions of the ending of the relationship, such as a confirmation that the client elected not to appeal a final order;

D. Address the status of fees and payment.

Non-engagement letters are also important. If a potential client does not hire the lawyer and does not sign the engagement agreement, or, if the lawyer declines the representation without preparing an engagement agreement, it is advisable to confirm this fact in a letter with the following elements:

A. Using simple, clear language, state that you are not accepting the case and will not be the lawyer for the individual;

Appendix 9 (Continued)

B. You may or may not want to explain why, but if you state a reason, it is best to be straight forward;

C. Resist the urge to comment on the merits of the case. In fact, you may want to state that the fact that you are declining the case is not a reflection on the merits of the case;

D. Where appropriate, encourage the person to seek other counsel, but unless it is obvious, avoid giving advice on any time limitation that may be applicable;

E. It may be appropriate to send the non-engagement letter by certified mail, return receipt, or in a manner to guarantee and document delivery. Retain the letter in a filing system so that you can find it if necessary years later.

1. Rule 1.5(b)
2. Rule 1.5(c)
3. D.C. Bar Legal Ethics Opinion 218, which should be read before drafting an arbitration provision.
4. D.C. Bar Rule XIII(a)
5. Rule 1.8 (i) – under certain circumstances, unpaid for work product may be retained by the lawyer.
6. D.C. Bar Legal Ethics Opinion 283.
7. Rule 1.15(d)
8. D.C. Bar Legal Ethics Opinion 103.
9. D.C. Bar Legal Ethics Opinion 345.

✄ ✄ ✄

More about Gary Richards

Besides the material in this book, you might be interested in the other services that Gary provides lawyers, law firms and bar associations.

Practice management services: Most law firms understandably spend little time on the art of managing an organization. Sometimes an outside, experienced and objective view can help.

- **Consulting:** Most law firms can benefit from an occasional tune-up in one operational area or another in order to remain efficient and effective. Gary consults on matters such as:
  - o Client relations
  - o Business Development [32]
  - o Legal Project Management
  - o Lawyer trust accounts (and associated Safe-keeping Rules)
  - o Managing billing and receivables
  - o Process Improvement
  - o Time Management for Support Staff
- **Custom and tailored programs for law firm retreats:**
  - o How to Improve Client Relations.
  - o How to Delegate Effectively to Lawyers and Non-lawyers
  - o How to Conduct Effective Client Meetings
  - o Setting Goals: for the Firm and Practice Groups

CLE workshops: At one time or another over the past 20 years, over 30 states with mandatory CLE have engaged

---

[32] Gary is a Principal in LegalBizDev. Through that organization he provides consulting, training and individual lawyer coaching on Legal Business Development and Legal Project Management.

Gary to develop and present programs for CLE credit, including ethics hours associated with these topics:

- o How To Get Work Done In A Law Firm
- o How To Reach Productive Agreements (Negotiating Skills)
- o Writing Skills For Lawyers
- o How To Keep Clients Happy

Coaching individual lawyers: Even the most experienced lawyers sometime need a tune-up! Coaching topics include but are not limited to various combinations of the following:

- o Personal Organization/Time Management.
- o Best Use of Your Firm's Timekeeping System
- o Managing Difficult Clients.
- o Business Development[33]
- o Setting Practice Goals

For more information

Google Gary- Search: *"Gary Richards LinkedIn-White Lake"*

Phone-248-705-7841   **Email**-gary1576@comcast.net

---

33 Offered through LegalBizDev using Jim Hassett's authoritative materials and concepts.

Printed in Great Britain
by Amazon.co.uk, Ltd.,
Marston Gate.